Why
SEA FISHING
with
Lighter Tackle Rocks

by

Lindsey Green

Publication Details

Lindsey Green

ISBN 978-0-9928824-5-7

978-0-9928824-5-7

Published by
Devon Fishing Guides
For any queries relating to this book, please email: info@devonfishingguides.co.uk

Dedication

This book is dedicated to my wife, Julie, and to my children, Anthony, Rebecca and Charlotte, all of whom have not only put up with a fishing-mad dad but have unwaveringly given their support to every project that I have ever undertaken.

Why SEA FISHING with Lighter Tackle Rocks

Table of Contents

Publication Details
Dedication
Table of Contents
Preface
Chapter One: The Marine Environment
Chapter Two: A Good Place to Start
Chapter Three: Light Rock Fishing
Chapter Four: Flounder Fishing
Chapter Five: Beach Fishing Continental Style
Chapter Six: First Steps Afloat
Chapter Seven: Pole Fishing
Chapter Eight: Pier Fishing Transformation
Chapter Nine – Spinning and Plugging
Chapter Ten – Fly Fishing

Preface

As I sit down to write, I first peer across the room to a picture hanging on the wall, where a lonely rock thrusts its way through the surface of a tranquil sea. Seagulls cluster on its sides while gannets glide effortlessly overhead, their mad, half-blinded eyes turned downwards in an endless search for sustenance. Seaweed fronds clump together where the rock meets the water and wave enticingly below where a myriad of tiny creatures scuttle, swim or inch their way cautiously forwards. About them as they do, so brightly coloured wrasse, handsome pollack and silvery bass prowl on all sides, both predator and prey locked in an endless quest for survival.

On the sand, at its base, plaice and other flatfish incuriously regard such species as gurnards, all of them hoping, perhaps, for a solitary prawn to momentarily reveal itself from cover. John dories drift listlessly by, ready in an instant to telescope their eager mouths about the smaller species upon which they continually predate. It is a beautiful scene, though I doubt that those same denizens would, were they able, describe their surroundings with quite such a romantic turn of phrase. For some it might be quite terrible so it is probably just as well that they are not blessed with the same powers of imagination that we humans take for granted.

But imagination, for me, is both crucial and central to the styles of fishing that I enjoy. Whether I am casting from the shore or drifting lazily by on a boat, so my mind's eye is ever turned downwards to the waters where I ply my art. I picture predators hungrily gathering around my vulnerable bait or, if they don't appear, then I use that same sense to try and determine what might be happening out of sight in the waters below. I run through different scenarios, constantly adapting both my methods and my tactics until I finally chance upon that moment of supreme satisfaction when my bait is consumed.

For me, fishing is not passive. I live for that moment when the rod bucks and arches in my hands, when the quarry that I have sought turns and flees, its every sinew straining as nature and instinct join forces against the sensations attempting to bend it to my will and its eventual capture. I love the fight - I am not bothered about eating what I catch – and, to a certain extent, there lives in me still the curious child that turned over rocks just to see what lay beneath. Each and every fish that I catch still stirs that curiosity, every struggle set against a background of wondering just what has taken my bait. What species is it? How big is it? Is it something new, something different to what I originally expected?

And there has never been a time quite like now in terms of opportunities to exercise this imaginative approach towards angling. We are living in a moment of our history when both our understanding of the marine environment and the sophistication of the tackle available to sea anglers enables us to pursue our quarry in a manner that would have turned our ancestors green with envy. We have tools and techniques available to us that our forebears could not even imagine, with space age materials producing ever lighter and more sensitive tackle that not only enables us to gain the best from every fish that we catch but also for the fish themselves to demonstrate exactly what they are capable of.

Every week I see new rods and reels brought upon the market while, at the same time, the flow of knowledge from continent to continent continually expands the range of tackle and techniques available to us. Love it or loathe it, the internet, combined with people's ability to experience fishing in far away places, has brought us a wealth of knowledge upon which we can easily draw. The result has been a boom in fishing knowledge and skills that have made sea angling today more exciting than it has ever been before. If only more people would take it up! I watch children play with clumpy, gross distortions of tackle in electronic games that seem to occupy them for hours while those same children turn their noses up at the thought of actually going fishing! It seems utterly ridiculous but, when you think about it, really quite predictable when you realise that we are living in an age when people want instant gratification.

In the electronic game, fish throw themselves upon the angler's bait with suicidal ferocity. The machine quivers and buzzes for a few seconds before an electronic voice drones that 'This one's huge!' Fishing's nothing like this, those children say to themselves, and so they play electronic versions without ever bothering to experience the real thing.

But, if they bothered, they would soon realise what a paltry imitation such games actually are. The thrill of a fish upon the line renders its electronic counterpart quite ridiculous, a stunted offering with nothing to recommend itself to a real angler. It is the merest echo of the truth that has enriched my life since I was a child. Now, with over 50 years of angling experience behind me, I still look forward to going fishing, to the contests that I most enjoy; where the fish that I catch are hooked and subdued with skill, perhaps, but not always, photographed and then released to fight another day.

In this book, I hope to share some of what makes me a passionate angler, the methods and the species that I most enjoy and, at the same time, offer you insights into ways in which you can learn to more quickly become a skilful angler. I cannot, and I will not, promise instant gratification. That is not possible and not even, to my mind, desirable. For me, a good fishing trip is one where you can whole-heartedly immerse yourself in the experience, which not only encourages a deeper understanding of what is going on but also provides a shortening of the process by which a fisherman, one who catches fish, is transformed into an angler, a person of noticeable skill who attains good results through his or her understanding of the quarry and the sport.

If that appeals to you, then that is wonderful. Stick with me and I will explain why sea fishing with lighter tackle rocks but, if it doesn't appeal, then that is fine too. It is just that this won't be the book for you.

Chapter One: The Marine Environment

When I was young, I had the great good fortune to spend a lot of my childhood within easy reach of the beach. Then, when we moved, I found myself with easy access to yet another. Four times this happened, with each and every one of them having a unique and distinctive character that I grew to love as I explored not only the beach nearest to where I lived but also all of its neighbours. I suppose I was also fortunate in living at a time when the young were able to roam without quite so much fear as to what might happen to them. I spent evenings, weekends and holidays blissfully turning over rocks or tramping over sand often miles from where I lived, blissfully unaware of, and untouched by, all of the considerations that would seriously worry a seven year-old's mother and father today.

For many anglers, casting from a beach is their favourite form of fishing. The trouble is, just where do you go?

It was another time but it enabled me to acquire an intimate knowledge of the foreshore that was close to where I lived, which has been a significant advantage throughout my angling career. I knew where the sandeels burrowed as the tide retreated, where the razorfish would be found in greater numbers, where the prawns would be largest and where I could dig for both white ragworms and lugworms at the same time. I knew where the crabs went to shed their shells and I soon discovered the most prolific of the local bait beds. After that it should come as no surprise that I ascertained, just as quickly, not only when but where the fish would be feeding as the tide turned and the sands were returned to the sea.

Good times and a different age perhaps but that knowledge has proved incredibly useful over the years. Even now, when faced with a new beach, the low tide has often seen me traipsing its length as I search for features that I can exploit.

And this is where knowledge starts to play a key part in the decisions that you are going to make. There are lots of people who go down to the beach, bait up and then throw their tackle as far out as they can in the hope that a fish will chance upon their bait. Why far out? Because, over the years, there has been a gradual brainwashing going on in the general angling populace that distance reigns supreme, the further out you can throw the lead the more macho you become, the more hard core the angler, the… well, you get the picture.

And it's codswallop. Sorry but it is. While distance casting is a very useful tool in the hands of a capable angler, it's not half as useful as knowing where you **should** be throwing the bait which is, surprise, surprise, where the fish are! What's the point in a two hundred yard cast when the fish are twenty yards out? Of course the reverse also applies but the key point is that if you can anticipate where the fish are going to be then you have a pretty good chance of catching them. Distance is useful, no doubt about it, but far more important is knowledge of where and when the fish will be feeding.

This is where low tide reconnaissance comes into play. Every feature that you can identify – and subsequently cast to – increases your chance of catching fish. So what do you look for?

Rockpools are an obvious feature, offering shelter to prawns, crabs and a host of small fish such as blennies, gobies, tiny pollack and wrasse. They can be a magnet for predators.

When you first go down to the shore, there will be big features that are easy to spot and there will be less obvious aspects that you will only find by examining the sand at your feet. At one of my local beaches, for example, there is a freshwater stream that runs underground, surfaces on the sand and then fans down to the sea, widening as it goes. This is the kind of mark that will see me there with the rising high tide, particularly at night, doing short casts into fairly shallow water. The reason for this is that it will attract sandeels, which will dig into the sand and then resurface with the incoming tide. The bass know this and, when the sandeels are present, will venture far closer to the shore than many people realise. I have seen them, when the sandeels emerge, still groggy from cover, hitting the shoals with as little as six inches of water to cover their backs. They have been so close that you could target them with a fly rod let alone a beachcaster!

I once saw a chap fishing this particular mark with a high power tournament rod. He was a really good caster, belting his bait out for hour after hour with sophisticated clip-down tackles that enabled him to cast as far as he possibly could. Of course he didn't catch anything, the fish were no further than thirty yards from the shore, completely unaware of the lead weight whistling over their heads on its trajectory to a barren stretch of sand where there was nothing to catch. The reason for this? There was nothing to attract any fish to it in the first place. When the fish come close to the shore, they are looking for food and if there is little or no food to find then they will move quickly on to where they do expect to find it.

Which is where the angler should be. If this particular gentleman had walked sixty yards to the left, he would have been casting into a huge bed of lugworms, which would have opened up the possibility of flatfish and other bottom feeders. If he had travelled one hundred yards to the right, he would have been putting his bait in the midst of one of the most prolific spots on the beach for razorfish and clams (gapers) which would have also opened up different sporting possibilities. As it was, he persisted with a style of fishing, and casting, which did not match the environment in front of him. It was good casting practice but that's all it was.

The moral of the story is simple. Don't get hung up on the issue of casting to the point where it blinds you to everything else. In the hierarchy of angling skills, I would personally put knowledge and watercraft above casting ability. That's not to say that it isn't important, it is, but casting is, after all, a delivery system to put your bait in front of the fish. If the fish aren't there then you need to rethink your strategy.

Just a bit further along this particular beach there is a pier. It's a real shame that they don't allow angling from it but that doesn't stop people in the know targeting it from both boat and shore. Basically every stanchion and girder provides an anchorage for seaweed, making it a little oasis of life in the midst of a sandy desert. Small fish and prawns use the seaweed for cover while crabs scuttle around its foundations, digging in next to the pillars whenever danger threatens or when it is time for them to hide away and shed their shells.

It is basically a smorgasbord for predators. Mackerel, garfish, pollack and bass pursue the smaller fish around it – enabling boat anglers to target them at the top of the tide - while bottom dwelling species such as gurnards take up station where the currents drop the food that they are expecting to find. Nor are they being unreasonably optimistic since the shape of the pier deflects the current, building up sandbanks and hollows where food being swept along in its grip will settle to the bottom. The local fish get to know these dining hotspots and anticipate when they are likely to be productive. The trick is for anglers to do the same so that they can place their baits in the midst of such feeding zones at exactly the right time, in which case they are very likely to catch.

Some very big bass roam around this particular pier with June and July offering a really good chance of catching a specimen fish. At this time they are there because there is an explosion of peeler crabs, crabs that are shedding their old shells to reveal soft new velvety exoskeletons that have yet to harden. During this time they offer hungry bass a delicious mouthful that is hard to resist, particularly if it is a big, juicy offering apparently just lying there in plain sight. Alternatively it might be a soft-backed crab that is lashed to a hook with a rubber band. It can move around, adding movement to help entice a predator, but it will be tethered in the close vicinity of the lead weight that forces it to maintain its position, right where it may not want to be but exactly where the angler does want it to be.

Of course you can't fish from the pier itself but that doesn't stop you donning waders and casting to it from the shore, particularly if you take up position on the opposite side to the main force of the current. If it is travelling right to left, I fish on the left and vice versa, basically doing what the fish are doing and taking advantage of the shape of the pier, letting it funnel or deflect the current to make their lives just that little bit easier.

At the opposite end of the beach there is a harbour, albeit one that almost dries out on the biggest of the spring tides. Its base is rich with seaweed and cover, with the walls offering sanctuary to countless thousands of prawns. Meanwhile, scurrying inwards and outwards with the rising and the falling tides, huge numbers of shrimps take advantage of the plethora of food available within the harbour's embrace, just as large swathes of lugworms take up residence on its sandy bottom. Countless crabs sidle along the harbour walls, providing hours of entertainment for the holidaymakers dropping their baited crablines in their pursuit, while mullet cruise in with the rising tide, ever on the lookout for scraps of bread and other food dropped overboard by the boat owners chatting away on their moorings.

Mind you, in the Summer, if you have a chance, I would suggest that you take a few minutes and keep an eye on just what those same boat owners throw over the sides of their vessels. A lot of them have been mackerel fishing, often gutting their catch and throwing the innards into the water. During the season, the mullet gain a taste for the softer parts of these offerings with the liver, in particular, becoming a favourite bait amongst anglers in the know.

On one occasion, a young blue shark came in with the tide, doing no harm to anybody, and cruised amongst the boats, keeping up this patrol for weeks. No-one I spoke to managed to put two and two together, which seemed to me ridiculous. It wasn't there because it was bored of its customary scenery, it was there for all the fish heads and other waste being dumped into the harbour. As far as it was concerned it was soup kitchen for sharks, getting its head down for the free offerings that were so conveniently, and so regularly, appearing.

At the side of the harbour, there is a boulder-strewn cove offering lots of cover and some very large rockpools. Just like the pier, this location is rich in small fish, crabs and prawns but, in addition, it offers a variety of rock-hugging or burrowing shellfish. Conger eels lurk or roam in the hollows amongst the boulders and each rising tide sees bass and pollack venture close in their perpetual quest for food. Of course the rough nature of the ground makes it a veritable snare for anglers' tackle but there are ways around this. They are not foolproof but they do minimise tackle losses so that trips become both practical and manageable.

The same logic applies wherever you find rockpools with one of the best areas to target being the sand around their edges, especially if this leads to broken patches of rocks between which predators can cruise at their leisure. Any prawn or peeler crab that ventures into such open spaces at the top of the tide – and they do – is taking a chance that may well end in personal disaster.

Especially if they are attached to an angler's hook.

Of course sometimes, particularly if you are away on holiday, you may not have time to do a low water reconnaissance and just want to go fishing. There are also beaches which seem pretty featureless and, despite the tides, don't dry out very much. These are harder to read, making it much more difficult to build up a comprehensive dossier on the way that they are likely to fish.

Despite that, there are still things that you can do. Big features will still be pretty obvious – rock formations, piers, harbours, groynes to deflect and break up the pull of the tide – and you can always vary both your bait and the distance that you cast. However, if it is an area that you are going to regularly fish, then get in the habit of taking a notebook with you. You can use this to build up a picture of successful marks, rigs, baits and distances that will gradually become more and more useful.

There are also other things that you can do, such as reading the waves. This is a skill that many anglers never really bother to research and this is a pity because it can give you clues into both the depth of water and the topography of the beach. It's also not that hard to acquire though it does take a bit of thinking about at first.

In some ways, wave behaviour can be thought about in terms of a man running forward. His head and his feet are travelling at the same speed and everything is going smoothly. Then, all of a sudden, he trips over an obstacle. His feet are slowed - held back by increased friction – but his head is still moving forward at speed. As a result he pitches forward. If he's unlucky, he will fall over completely.

Now apply this same logic to waves. When the wave length is less than the depth of water over which the wave is travelling, then there is no friction to worry about and everything is moving forward at the same speed, giving the wave a well-rounded swell. Then the wave starts to meet shallower water. The water travelling beneath it meets increased friction from the sand or other bottom and the wave begins to peak.

This starts to happen when the depth of water is roughly half the length of the wave.

As the water gets shallower, the water at the top of the wave begins to travel in front of the water at the bottom, becoming a breaker. Eventually this falls completely forward and the result is the shallow water waves that complete the wave's passage to shore.

Breakers form when the depth of water is less than half the length of the wave. Hopefully the diagram should make the idea a bit clearer.

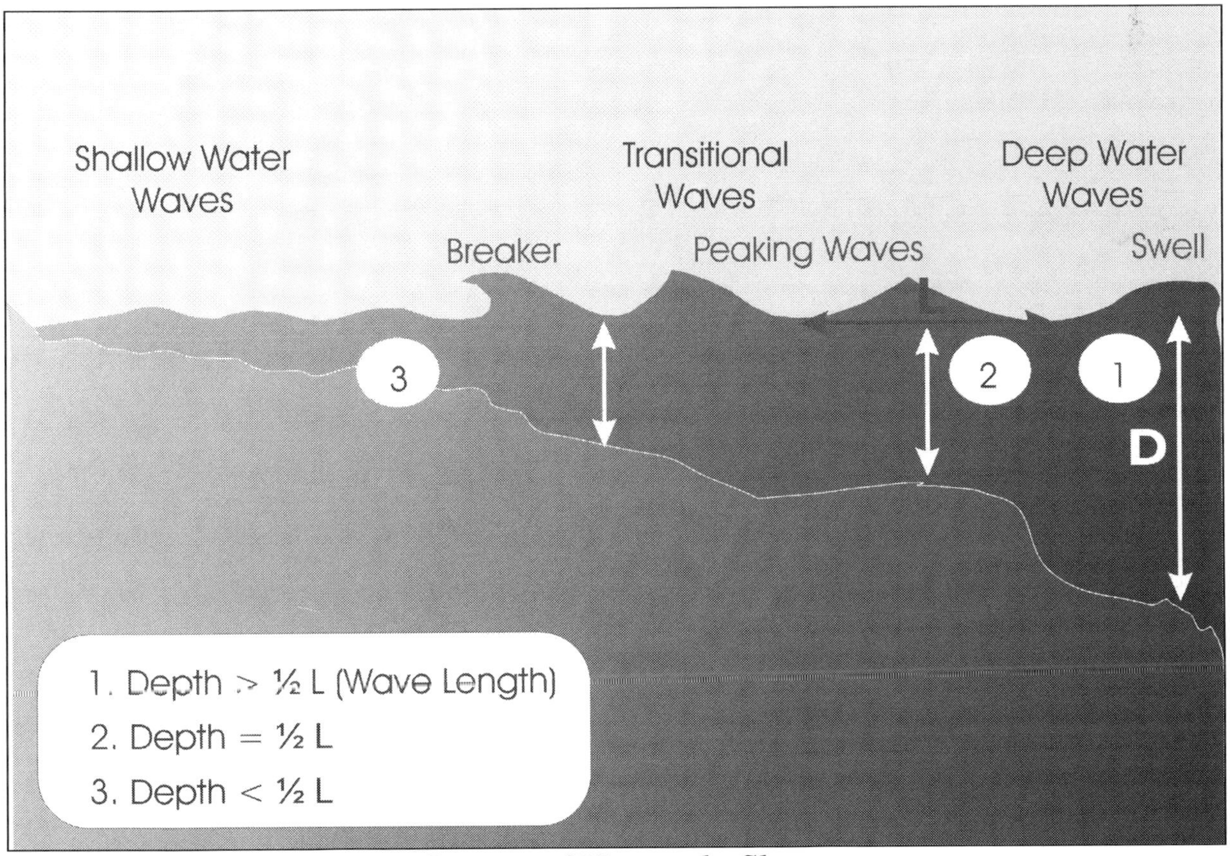

Passage of Wave to the Shore

So how does this help us? Well, if you look at lot of beaches you will see that the waves do not coast uniformly over their surface. At a mark close to where I live, waves cresting from left to right hit a spot where they smooth back into a swell before reforming into a crest some fifty yards later. This is because there is an area of deeper water beneath them, which affects the waves' shape. What it also does is become a holding ground for food particles that are dropped by the current, creating a potential feeding ground for the fish. They soon become aware of its presence and it is probably one of the best spots on the beach.

At the end of beaches, there are very often rocky headlands or outcrops that give way into deeper water. These can be really good fishing marks. They have a resident head of wrasse and, in season, will draw bass, bream and a host of other predators on the lookout for food, not least of which will be the ever popular mackerel and garfish. You can fish these in several ways but your prey will change depending on your tactics. If you can find patches of rock in the midst of the sand, casting onto those rocks will provide a different mix of fish to casting onto the sand around them. At one spot that I fish, for example, there is a six foot radius of rock that is a holding ground for bream, at least in the Summer. Miss it and you don't catch the bream but you may catch dragonets, pout and small flatfish such as dabs.

Rocky headlands, regardless of where they are in the world, are usually very good spots to fish. This one is in Portugal but it still held corkwing wrasse and bream, providing some very good sport at the top of the tide.

If you are lucky enough to live near to a major headland, such as Hopes Nose in Torbay, then this opens up all sorts of possibilities. It is also quite interesting because your strategies and methods will change with the seasons. It can be a bit of a trek down but it is usually well worth it. In the Summer, you can float fish for mackerel, garfish, bass, wrasse and pollack, amongst others, while the Autumn brings in flatfish, making bottom fishing much more interesting and enjoyable. Winter brings the chance of cod, albeit with the reality of dogfish and whiting, while the Spring offers the chance of wrasse, herring and mackerel before seeing the full return of the Summer species.

And, with the range of tackles and methods available today, these are just the tip of the iceberg. You can experiment with light rock fishing tackle, fly fishing, hybrid tackles, which are a combination of lure and bait, poles, spinning, plugging, top-surface methods and a variety of float fishing methods designed to maximise the sport available from every one of the fish that you catch. The key is that you can reach deep water with fairly short casts which, in turn, means that you can often get away with really light tackle.

As far as I am concerned, the lighter the better. I have lost count of the number of times when I have seen heavy tackle used to unceremoniously drag fish ashore with little or no resistance. One chap watched me play a fish on the ultra light rod that I was using – a 12 foot float rod designed specifically for casting sea fishing floats – and looked puzzled when I finally netted it. "It's not very big, is it?" he said. "The way it was fighting, I thought that it was going to be a lot bigger than that."

Considering the fact that his rod was a telegraph pole by comparison to mine, that was hardly surprising. The fish that he was catching were simply outgunned by the tackle that he was using. Trouble is, a lot of people do the same thing, using cheap, often awful tackle which is not only unsporting but unnecessary given the advances in technology today. Far better to give them a sporting chance, especially since you can pick up some really nice tackle, especially light tackle, at excellent prices. Today, it doesn't have to be expensive to be good. There are some real bargains to be had.

Breakwaters and piers offer the same kind of exciting possibilities that you get with headlands. However their accessibility makes it easier to target bigger fish such as conger eels, which will live wherever there is a craggy bottom or a structure with stony sides and plenty of cover. They are also arguably more gentle places to try fishing at night, with the mix of rocks close in and sand or mud further out opening up a wide range of target species.

For me, one of the greatest gifts of angling is the unexpected, such as this superb three bearded rockling caught by Tony Searle off Brixham Breakwater.

One of my favourite spots is Brixham Breakwater, which you can explore for a week with different methods and still find out something new at the end of it. It offers access to deep water, is inhabited by lots of different species and, for the angler prepared to experiment, is an absolute gem of a place to visit.

Piers and breakwaters are superb places to try out all sorts of different methods and tackles. Here I am using an ultralite spinning rod from America against mackerel and garfish. The rod cost less than £20.

For now, I think that's probably enough to be going on with. Within the chapters that follow, I will break down the ideas behind the trips that I will be using as examples so that you can see why I adopted the approach that I did. I don't want to make things too complicated, especially since, as I am getting older, I find myself steering away from complicated super rigs and streamlining wherever possible. I still make a lot of things myself, some of which I am going to share because I find that catching fish on things that you have made yourself adds another dimension to the sport, but on the whole I find myself turning more and more towards a lighter and less cluttered approach.

I suppose that's just the way that I am progressing. However, as you progress, so you will find that some things become second nature, things which most anglers don't mention because they take them for granted. Take, for example, night fishing. During the dark hours, fish will come much closer in than they would in the day so closer casts, sometimes as little as ten yards from the shore, will still catch fish. You will also gain a sensitivity to the tides, especially when you find your best catches almost always falling on a big spring tide rather than the smaller neaps. These, and all sorts of other things, you will discover on your journey to becoming a true angler. However, in the meantime, I am going to move on to some of the basics that will, hopefully, start to steer you in the right direction.

Chapter Two: A Good Place to Start

There are lots of starting points that I could explore but, for me, one of the most exciting has got to be float-fishing. It was one of the first things that I ever tried and, even now, I still look forward to doing it again. There's just something about it, something about that moment when your float suddenly dips and then disappears from view. You haven't got long to react – pause and the fish will usually be gone – but this just adds to the thrill. You know you have got to be quick if you are going to succeed, which increases the sense of satisfaction when you find yourself not only hooking but playing a decent fish on the line.

Your tackle is also not going to break the bank. There are a number of rods and reels on the market that will do an excellent job without costing an arm and a leg in the process. Suitable outfits also tend to be fairly simple to use, making casting effortless and helping each fish to put up a game struggle as they fight to escape. I love it and, from the hundreds of people that I have helped over the years, I have seen just how much enjoyment simple float fishing can give.

Of course first of all you are going to need to get a rod and reel. For the rod, I would suggest a nine to eleven foot long spinning rod, medium weight, capable of casting weights from 12 to 42 grams. I like using lighter still but, for someone just starting out, it is probably better to give yourself a bit of a safety margin. Then, for the reel, I would stick to a fixed spool no bigger than 4000 size and preferably 3000 size to better match the rod. It doesn't really matter whether the reel is front or rear drag (the drag allows the line to come off the reel under tension) but rear drag is easier to get to when you are actually in the middle of a fight.

The next thing to do is to load the reel with twelve to fifteen pounds breaking strain line. For this, I would always stick to clear nylon monofilament. Some people like using braid – I think it is absolutely brilliant for boat fishing – but I don't like it for float fishing. Its total lack of stretch makes it extremely unforgiving for striking, giving you no leeway at all in terms of the precision of the strike (an upwards pull on the rod to set the hook against a taking fish). You have to be exactly on time with a precisely timed and suitably forceful sweep of the rod, making sure that you apply just the right amount of pressure since pulling too hard will snatch the bait away from the fish. Nylon is much more forgiving than braid in this respect and, with a coating of Mucilin line floatant, will float on the surface to make striking even easier and more likely to succeed.

Mucilin line floatant is, for me, a must-have accessory for float fishing. If you haven't got it, your line will sink, creating a large underwater bow between the tip of the rod and the float. When you strike, most of the force will be used up in bringing the line tight against the friction of the water, making hooking the fish much more difficult. If you are using floatant, then your line will sit comfortably on the surface of the water so that you can see what is going on. Then, when you strike, most of your force goes into hooking the fish rather than pulling the line to the surface.

For floats, I would stick to the West country sliding, cigar-style models. These have great buoyancy while their slim diameter makes pulling them underwater nice and easy for the fish. This gives you a clear visual cue to strike and also gives you a fraction of a second longer before the fish suspects that something is wrong and spits the hook out. With chunkier models there is more resistance so the fish tend to get rid of the hook faster, making accurate striking just that little bit more difficult.

In regard to actual size, I like to use floats that are about eight inches (20.3 cm) long and which are weighted by ¾ ounce (21 gram) drilled bullet leads. The diagram on the next page shows you how to set the tackle up.

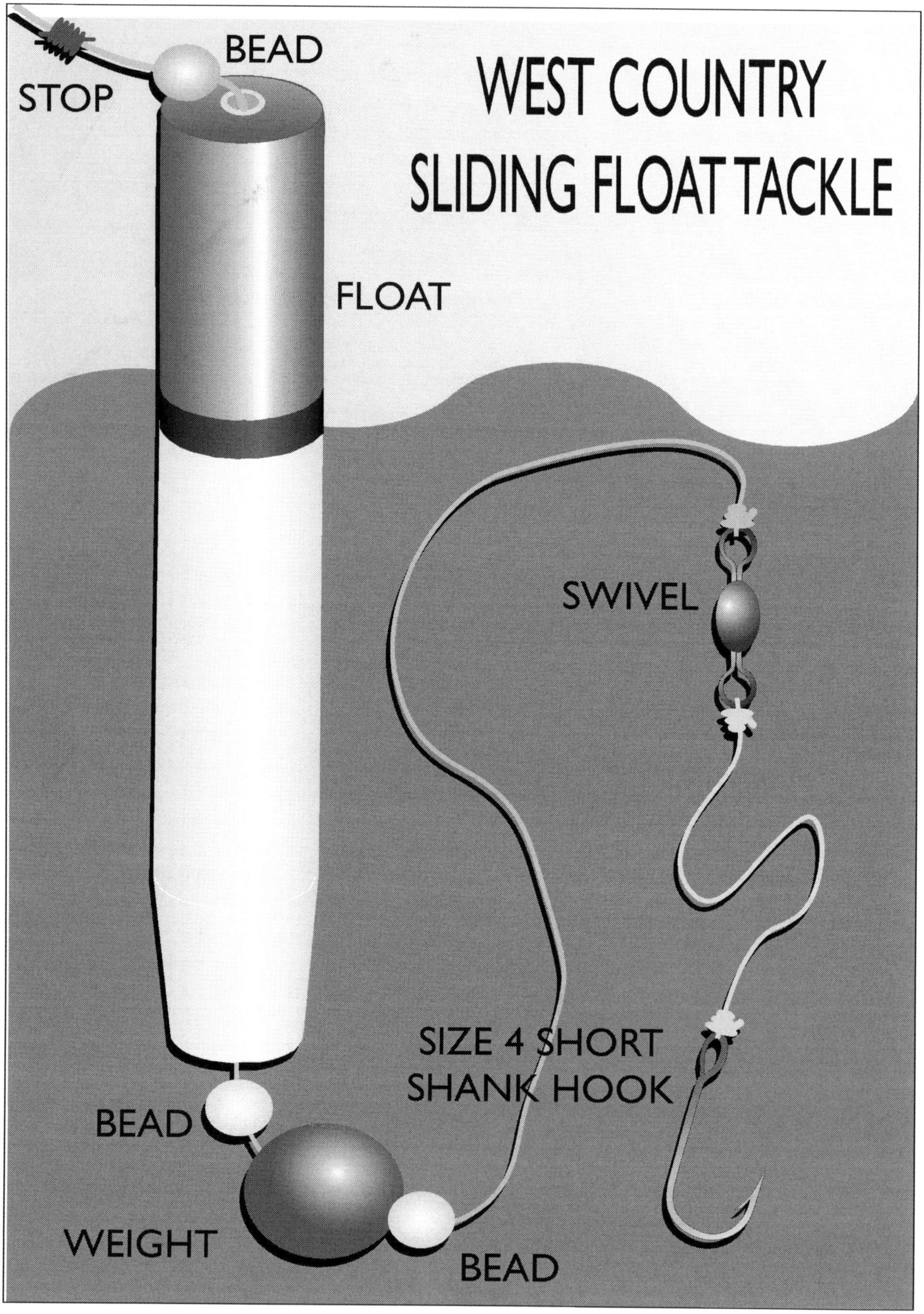

Now there is nothing wrong with using the tackle just as it is – most people do – but there is one thing that I like to do that is just a little bit different. I put my weights on a piece of stainless steel wire, then twist the first end into the shape of a plain round eye before doing the same to the other end, except this time I attach a swivel. It takes a couple of minutes with a pair of mole grips and pliers but it both saves me money and gives me added confidence in my tackle.

The reason for this is the friction generated by the weight sliding up and down on the line. It frays it, which makes it weaker. By putting the weight on the wire, it has a much harder surface to rub against which won't give way under sudden pressure. I have seen a lot of people lose decent fish on float gear, usually because the weight has abraded the line to the point where it is weakened and snaps, at which point they lose both the fish and all of the tackle to which it is attached. That doesn't happen if you put the lead on a wire link.

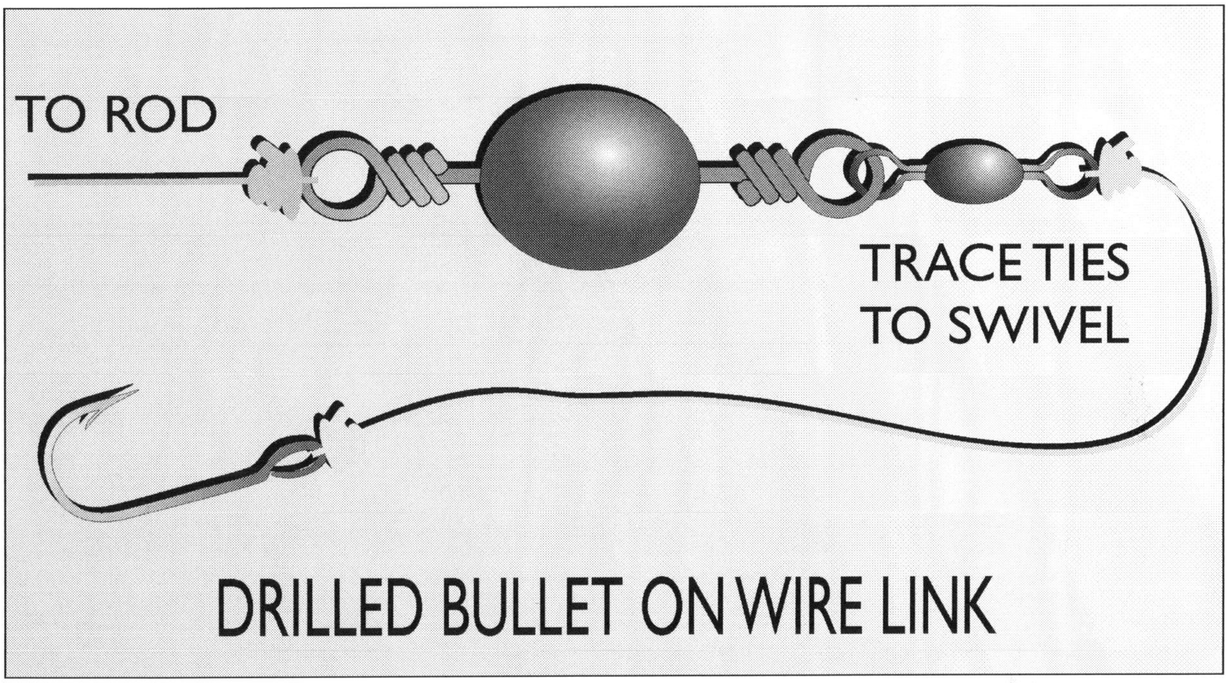

The trace, which is a length of weaker line some three to four feet long, is tied to the swivel because, when you are float fishing, most of the time you will be using baits like live sandeels or strips of mackerel. These spin when you reel in so your trace gets more and more twisted until it is unfishable. The swivel, as long it is the right size, prevents that. However don't be tempted to put on a massive swivel to be sure that it twists okay. Actually the opposite happens. If the swivel is too big, the thin line that you use for your trace won't be stiff enough to turn it. Your line will still end up with lots of kinks in it. A smaller swivel, on the other hand, will turn with the line and stop this happening.

For my trace I like to use 8 to 10 pounds breaking strain fluorocarbon. This is a clear line, somewhat more expensive than nylon monofilament, which is very hard to spot underwater. I find that I have a lot more bites using it than people around me who aren't.

To put the tackle together, you are going to need to learn a couple of knots. The first one that I would suggest is the grinner knot, which is neat, strong and very small. It will cover most of the eventualities that you are ever going to face although, as your experience grows, you might like to learn a few others along the way for specialist jobs. Fair enough but, for now, I would suggest that this is something to worry about later. For the moment, the grinner will do the job superbly.

The other knot that you will need to know how to tie is the stop knot. This regulates the depth at which you are fishing. Slide it towards the reel and your tackle fishes deeper. Slide it towards the float and your tackle will be shallower.

When I target mackerel, I usually start at fourteen foot deep and then adjust as I go along. If the fish don't respond, I tend to go deeper first and then, if that doesn't work, shallower. For garfish I will start at about ten feet deep. Some people like to start at around six feet but, over the years, I have found that bigger garfish tend to be that little bit deeper.

Grinner Knot

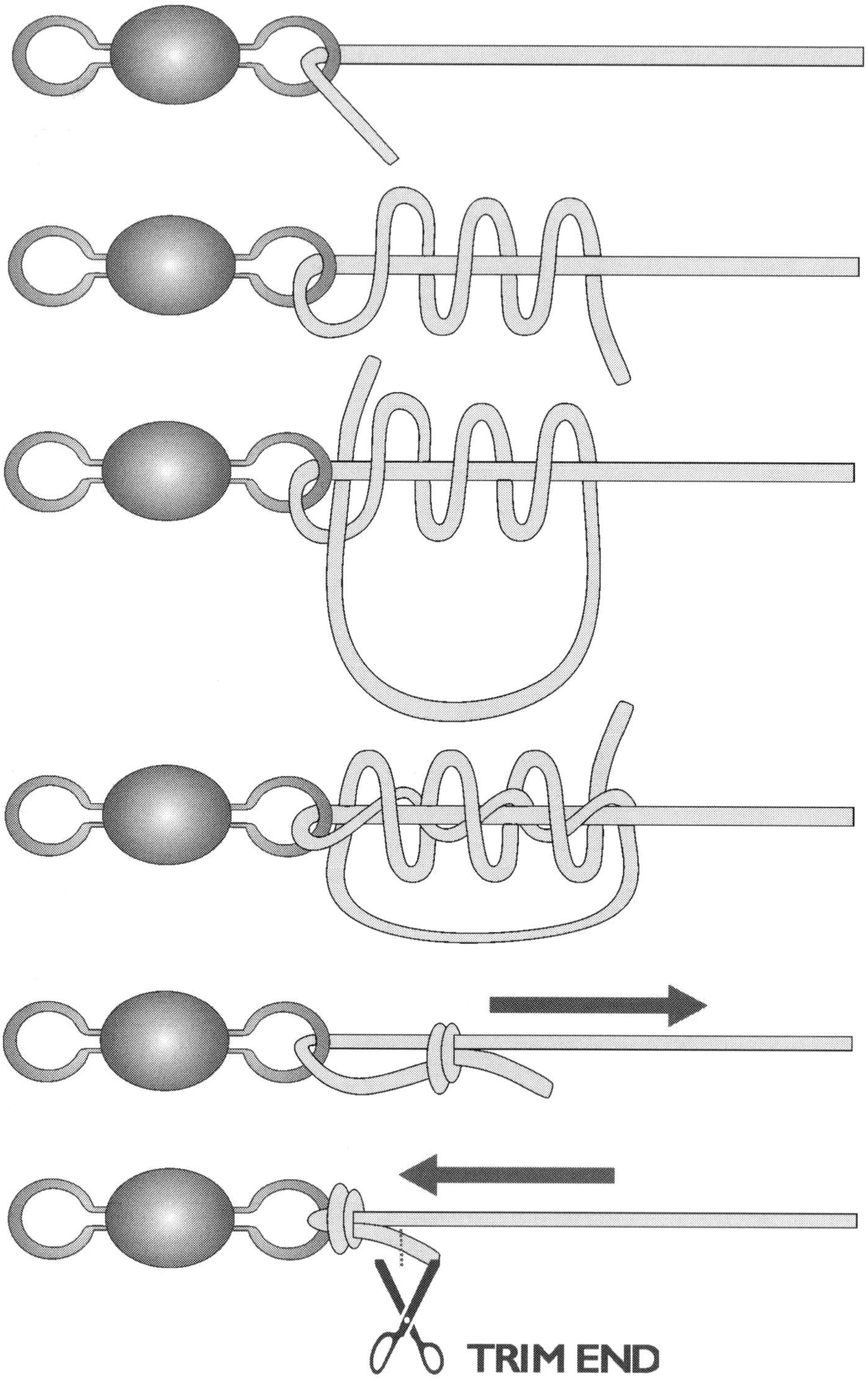

1. Start by threading on your swivel (hook etc.) and passing through about 15 cms (6 inches) of line.

2. Twist the spare end about the main line three times for thicker diameters or four times for finer ones.

3. Pass the spare end through the first twist next to the eye of the swivel (top to bottom). Pull the coiled and singled strands into a loop with the doubled strands on the right.

4. Coil the spare end about the doubled strands for a further three or four turns - three times for thicker diameters or four times for finer ones - working from top to bottom, moving away from the eye.

5. Lubricate the knot and pull on the spare end, which will move the knot up and away from the eye of the swivel. (It will shrink in size as you do.)

6. Pull on the main line to fully tighten the knot. It will slide down next to the eye and form, if you have done it right, a very small and tidy knot. Trim the spare end about 4 millimetres away from the coils and you are done.

Stop Knot

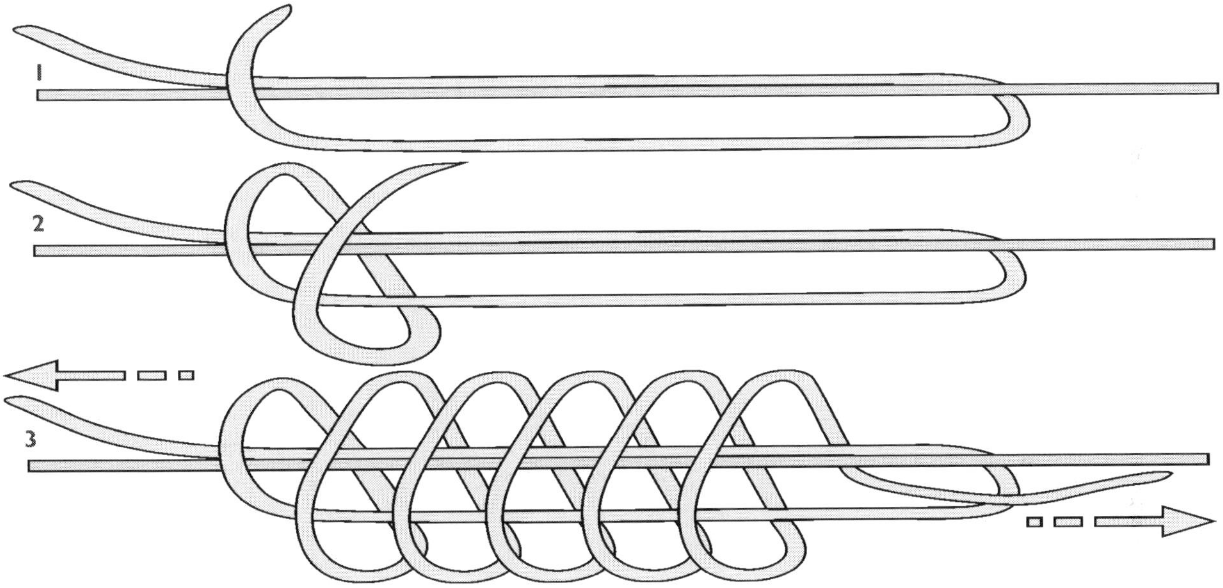

1. Make a loop in a length of nylon and lay it next to your main line. When you first try this out, it is probably best to give yourself about an eighteen inch (45 cm) length although you will find, once you have got this down pat, that you will probably be able to get away with a foot.

2. Pull one end of the loop longer than the other side. Turn it back on itself and coil it around both sides of the loop and the main line. Make five turns around both.

3. Tuck the end through the eye of the loop and then pull tight – slowly - from both ends. As the knot gets smaller, wet the line to stop it being damaged by friction. (This is a good habit to get into since you should always lubricate any knot before you pull it tight.) Trim to finish, leaving about half a centimetre on both sides of the knot. Don't trim too close just in case the bead above the float slides over it, in which case the float would go over it too and you would be fishing on the bottom instead of midwater!

Once you have set up your tackle, the last thing that you will need to do is to get your bait sorted out. There are a number of options here but a lot of people will use either strips of mackerel, strips of squid or sandeels, either live or frozen.

If you use mackerel, cut thin strips and slice them away from the majority of the flesh behind the skin. They should be about two millimetres thick since you want them to move with the current not just lay bunched up in a thick chunk on the hook. Done properly, they should wave enticingly which they won't do if you leave all of the flesh on. Another tip will depend on the season. When mackerel first appear in the Spring, they will normally be feeding on very small sandeels. If your strips are too large, they will not be consistent with the food that the shoals are targeting so they will probably be rejected. Cut them really fine with an equally small (less than 1 centimetre) width for better early season sport.

Keep the same principle in mind when you cut up squid. If you use catering squid, you may well find that the depth of the flesh is fine for use as the width of the strip, meaning that you can cut a lot of very fine strips out of a single tube. You won't be able to do this with calamari. If you use the latter, you will also need to scrape the pink skin off to reveal the white flesh underneath.

Sandeels are a deadly bait for mackerel with three methods of hooking available. The first, which I use only if they are dead, is to hook them through the front of the eye socket, taking care not to puncture the eye itself. The second is to hook them, with a short shank, light wire hook, just behind the eye and the third, for which I use a fine wire, long shank hook, is to thread the hook through the mouth, out of the gills, then turn and nick the stomach flesh lightly.

The diagrams should make the second and third methods clear.

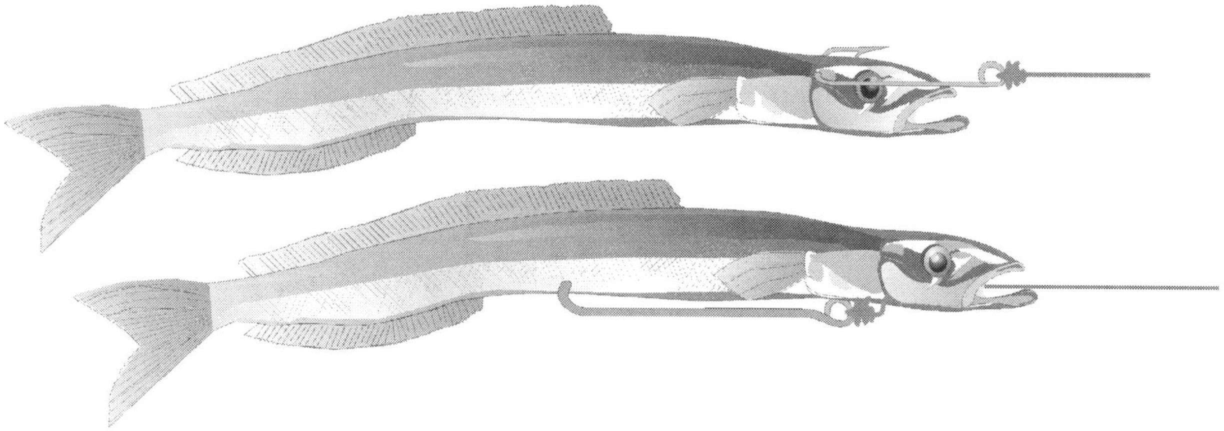

Don't forget something to store your bait in through the day. If you use a bait pot, you will probably get away with this on its own during the early part of the season and Winter but, as the Summer warms up, you will find your bait starting to go off very quickly. It is best to have a cool bag with ice packs in it so that you can put your pot away whenever you are not using it. If you don't, you will soon find it turning and covered in flies and wasps, the latter of which can be really persistent and annoying!

So much for theory! Quite enough to take in for now so let's go fishing, seeing if we can't put things into perspective.

The first trip that I have decided to share with you was one to Brixham Breakwater in Torbay. It was late April and the weather was decidedly unencouraging, being both a little bit chilly and on the windy side with a breeze coming in from the sea. Still, I was fed up of being cooped up at home so I sorted out my tackle, wrapped up warmly and took myself off for an afternoon's fishing.

Early Spring, it is important to take a few extra minutes to sort out your clothing. I didn't want to be encumbered with a storm suit – I would have got too hot, too quickly – so I built up a few base layers and kept a warm hat to hand to keep the chill off my ears. I always find that I am much more comfortable with a lined hat to keep my head warm. Without it, I tend to get cold much more quickly, especially when there is a bit of a breeze.

Arriving at the Breakwater, I saw that the outside was choppy and the water discoloured. Not things that would have worried me too much mid-summer but, at this time of the year, I figured that the baitfish upon which the mackerel would be feeding would be inside the shelter of the harbour, probably nestling a little way off the rocks where the water was a bit calmer. High tide was due in a couple of hours so I had plenty of time to walk towards the end and then take station on the inside, just back a little way from the end itself. Here the water was being sheltered by the shape of the breakwater, which was creating an interesting little spot where the waves were coming round the corner and then gradually fading away.

For me, this looked like a spot where food would accumulate quite quickly, which always grabs my attention. Find the food and you'll find the fish so I settled down, tackled up and pottered out my float. I wasn't too worried about distance so a gentle overhead thump put me right in the midst of the area that I wanted to explore.

If you're new to fishing, the 'overhead thump' is the simplest form of cast. It won't reach the same distances as pendulum and off-the ground casts, more sophisticated techniques for more experienced anglers, but it will cast far enough to catch plenty of fish. It is also the only practical cast for float fishing since spinning rods are not designed for these other styles of casting. They were developed for fishing at range and for the tournament field, for putting heavy weights massive distances with heavy beachcasters.

To start the overhead thump, you rotate the rod to an upside-down position so that your fixed-spool reel is on top of the rod with about three to four feet of line between the rod tip and the weight. I'm right handed so I put my left hand at the bottom of the rod and my right hand about the reel seat. I split my middle fingers around the reel stem, which means that I have a good, solid grip upon the rod.

The reason that the reel is upside-down at this time is because, during the cast, your hand is going to go from facing up to facing down and so will the rod. If the reel isn't above the blank, your wrist will have to twist and you will lose power, grip and flow.

Instead of every part of the cast flowing smoothly from one point to another, the sequence becomes jerky, which interrupts the smooth transition of power. What you want is for the rod to compress then straighten smoothly, transferring that energy to the lead to fire it out where you want it to go. Start with your hands and the reel in the wrong position and you make this much more difficult, losing distance and increasing strain upon your wrist.

Your end finger traps the line against the rod so that you can take off the bale arm. Line won't spill from the spool if that is on. I then take off the anti-reverse, rotate the bale arm to a position where it won't accidentally trip during the cast, and then re-engage the anti-reverse so that the bale arm is trapped in position.

The Actual Cast

1. Footing and stance is important so I position my left foot forwards with my right foot behind it, shifting a little to make sure that I am both comfortable and balanced. For beginners, it is a good idea to point your left foot to where you want the weight to land. The natural set of your shoulders will, when it comes time to let the line go and release the lead, help to make sure that the rod is pointing straight in line with the toes of your left foot. This will aid accuracy.

I also start with the rod held high so that I can give it a little swing to start to compress the rod.

2. Give the rod a little swing away from you. My left arm comes up to the same height as my right with my hands set at slightly above shoulder height.

3. My left arm now pulls down at the same time that my right arm pushes forward. It's a similar motion and grip as if you were trying to hit a high target with a long-handled sledgehammer. Both arms need to contribute speed and power so that this part of the cast is smooth and balanced. The most common mistake is that the right arm does most of the work while the left arm merely guides. Get both arms working properly and you will add considerable distance to the cast.

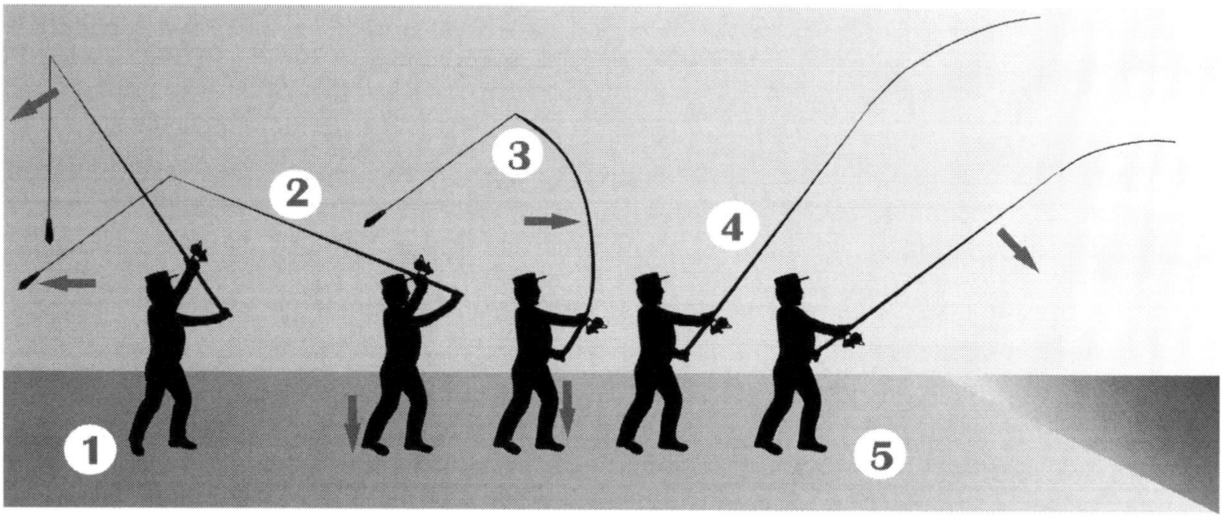

4. When the rod is pointing to a position that is both high and in front of me – somewhere between one and two o'clock – I let the line go. Too early and the lead goes high and not so far. Too late and the lead crashes into the ground at your feet.

5. As the lead descends, I follow it down with the rod. My aim is to keep the line nicely tunnelled in the rings to remove as much friction from the cast as possible. If you keep the rod high, the increased friction as the weight drops will lead to a shortened cast.

If you are left-handed, try the whole procedure with your arms in the reverse position. It may take a little practice but you should get the hang of it fairly quickly.

Common mistakes to watch out for include:

- One arm doing most of the work;
- Letting go of the rod with one hand, usually the one holding the bottom of the handle. This is a sure sign that one arm is doing all of the work and could even lead to letting go of the rod altogether;
- Releasing the line too early or too late;
- Casting anywhere but straight in front of you. Look at where your left foot is pointing and visualise the lead impacting the water straight in front of your toes.

On this particular day, I decided to start float fishing with my depth set at around seventeen feet. Since it was a bit on the chilly side, I went a little bit deeper than my usual starting point of fourteen feet, especially since it was also a spring tide, giving me a little bit more leeway in regard to the depth of water. (You get much higher high tides with a spring tide and much lower low tides. The water comes in a long way but it goes a long way out too. Most of the time, I concentrate on fishing the high tides in this period and ignore the lows, which can be difficult to fish.)

I was joined by my friend, Sid Bradley, and we had a few small mackerel, nothing really to speak of but enough to put a bend in the rod. Then Sid had a bite that was definitely not a mackerel. His float started to lift, tottered slightly on its side and then vanished underwater, only to reappear a second later when he was a little slow on the strike and missed.

To me, this argued the possibility of a garfish. They will often play with the bait, rise with it and then, mercurially, decide that they really want it after all and go for it much more whole-heartedly. Since my float was about fifteen feet away from Sid's, directly in the path of any fish travelling in that direction, I tightened up my line and waited.

Some years, not every year by any means, some really big garfish appear in the last week of April and the first three weeks of May. With the conditions as they were, I had a feeling that it might be something special.

Seconds can pass very slowly when you are anticipating something good coming along. As it was, I had just got to the point where I had decided that nothing was going to happen after all, when my float vanished so quickly that it left a hole in the water. Tensed for this to happen, I reacted instantly, sweeping my rod up with a lunge that was swiftly turned into a satisfying bend. The creature was hooked and, from the force of its dive, was a good one. Now we only had to find out what it was.

Keeping pressure on, I turned the fish away from a crab pot rope towards which it was heading and then steered it where I wanted it to go. It cut and ran, shaking its head, but, unusually for a garfish, tried to stay deep until I tightened down on it further, forcing it up from the depths to the point where we could both see it. It was certainly a garfish, possibly the biggest one that I had seen, so Sid dashed to the landing net and dipped it in the water, ready for when I brought it to the side.

Not that this would be straight away. I was testing out a new rod, which I had loaded with eight pounds breaking strain line and six pounds breaking strain trace. The test curve of the rod – basically the amount of pressure that can be loaded onto the blank without breaking it – was a paltry six ounces so I had to work to get back every yard of line that the fish seemed so intent upon taking back out again. I could feel every shake of its head, every lunge for the depths and it is this, this feeling of being so connected to the fish, that is why light tackle is so exciting.

On a heavy rod, I would have simply dragged it ashore and where's the fun in that? It's like turning up for a duel with a cannon. Your opponent is severely overmatched and can do little to make things more interesting. On light tackle, however, you have to work to bring him in and this, for me, makes things much more interesting.

By now, my opponent was beginning to tire and I was able to exert a little more pressure, eventually bringing him close enough to the side for Sid to be able to net. He made one last, half-hearted attempt to get away but it wasn't in him. I drew him back to the waiting folds of the knotless mesh (much kinder on the delicate scales of species like garfish) and Sid gently swept him from the water and onto the shore.

It was, as I had suspected, an absolute cracker of a garfish. Two pounds, four ounces and eight drams, a wonderful specimen and a new club record. I was seriously chuffed!

Sid moaned that it was really his fish and that he should have been the one to catch it. However he had to admit that he was a little bit late striking and his line, which had sunk, needed to be pulled to the surface before any of the force could be transferred to the hook and the fish. By contrast, I had treated my line with Mucilin so it was ready for immediate action when the garfish took hold of the bait.

A little thing, perhaps, but then it so often is with fishing. One small detail can make all the difference. It certainly did here. I was also using a light fluorocarbon trace while Sid was using heavier clear monofilament. With fluorocarbon much harder to see underwater, the bite that I had was much more confident and aggressive, giving me a better chance of setting the hook. By contrast, Sid's bite had been much more half-hearted.

Big garfish sometimes turn up in late April and early May, gathering in larger shoals before they spread out around the bay.

We fished on for a while longer, catching a few small mackerel in the process but without any sight of a second big garfish to soothe Sid's ruffled feathers. Not that he minded. We both had a great time and, even though it was my turn to catch a good fish on this particular day, he has had more than a few in his time.

Like most of my angling friends, we enjoy the banter and the companionship just as much as the fishing. Although, and I am sure that there is no truth in it, he does like to say that I only count aloud when I have caught the most fish. Apparently, if I am not 'winning', I go suspiciously quiet. Hum, I shall have to watch out for that…

Chapter Three: Light Rock Fishing

Looking back over a fifty year period of fishing, especially if you have gone out of your way to explore all sorts of different ideas and methods, it is easy to spot when things come along that are similar to previous incarnations. Sometimes the tackles and the ideas evolve into something genuinely new and sometimes old ideas resurface, are given off a dusting and then surrounded by hyperbole and marketed as the latest big thing to emerge in the world of sea fishing.

Light rock fishing is one area that combines both of these scenarios. The rods that are used are superb with a new, innovative design that enables you to catch reasonable fish on slender wands with the tiniest and most sensitive of tips. The lightness of the blank – the basic rod upon which the rings etc are mounted – enables even tiny fish to put up an interesting struggle. They are very different to what has gone before, even though, forty years ago, we had rods that did the same job, albeit not as efficiently and without the steely bend in the lower sections of the blank.

They weren't commercially available though. My friends and I used to make the ones that we used out of the blanks of fly fishing rods, which allowed us to cast tiny lures a reasonable distance. They were superb for when the mackerel were shoaling against the beaches, driving whitebait ashore as they hurled themselves into the midst of the panicked shoals, but they were floppy. We caught lots of fish where they could run, for example in places where there was virtually no cover, but when we tried them out on harbour walls, it was much more difficult. The rods lacked the backbone to coax the fish from cover so we lost a lot of tackle.

But we had a heck of a lot of fun in the process. At the time ABU produced a trigger grip handle that you could glue onto the lower end of a suitably light blank. Matched with a palm-sized baitcaster (closed face, not multiplier version) you had an outfit that cast very light lures or spinning tackle that we used to catch hundreds of pollack, mackerel and the occasional wrasse, even garfish if you used strips of bait instead of lures. Woolworths – remember them? - sold ridiculously fine lines that we used to great effect, one of my favourites being a gossamer stranded monofilament rated at ¾ lbs breaking strain. They also sold mini-pirks, tiny little metal lures weighing around ¼ oz, which mackerel and schoolie bass absolutely loved. Put the two together and we could cast a long way for the maximum amount of sport that it was then possible to experience, at least with what was available at the time.

One of the tackles that we used then – a tiny ball weight above a swivel with a little lure on the end of a three foot or longer trace – has since been rebranded as 'The Carolina Rig', but to us it was just a rig that we used for spinning with little lures. It was great for spinning where a constant retrieve, albeit varied in terms of speed and action, was called for and it is still just as effective today, particularly for pollack. We used to buy the smallest rubber eels that we could find with one of my favourites a little grey sandeel with a curly tail – Westenders, they were called, though a bit different to today's Westender bass lures - which pollack, bass and mackerel went nuts for.

Nowadays I still use this rig for spinning for pollack in particular though the range of lures available to mount on the hook has changed enormously from what was available in my youth, especially since I also make a lot of my own lures. (I won't go into this here although, if you are interested, I detail exactly how to do this in 'The Challenge of Inshore Boat Fishing', which is also available as a Kindle download.) The only real difference in the tackle is that today I mount the little drilled bullet leads on a wire mount, just like I do for float fishing and for the exact same reason. It protects the line from fraying and gives me confidence in my ability to land the fish that I hook. Without this link the line is weakened with every cast until it is likely to snap.

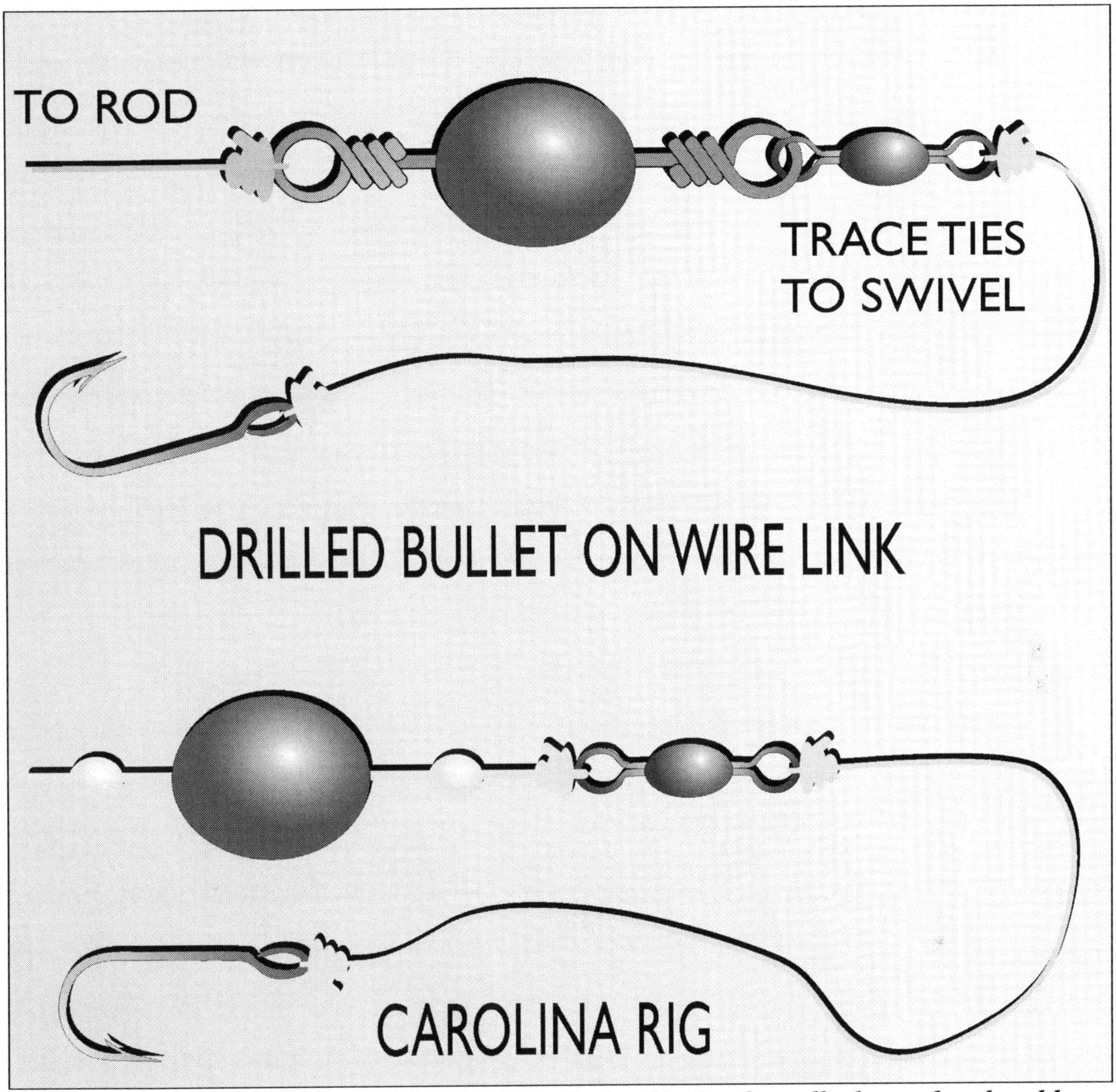

A dead easy rig to tie and one which is particularly effective for pollack, mackerel and bass. On the hook you can put on whatever lure takes your fancy. Small rubber eels are my favourites.

In the last twenty to thirty years, there has been a great deal of work done in the area of rubber and soft plastic lures, giving you an enormously wide choice. America spent decades looking at action, flavour and shape while Japan also looked at scent and attraction. Over here, amongst other things, we looked in particular depth at sandeels, with Alex Ingram producing the red gill, a devastating little lure that still catches its fair share of pollack, bass, coalfish and cod. Other British companies were also interested and the range of British lures then widened out to become imitations of many of the species preyed upon by our native predators.

The result is a range which will handle almost all species of fish, from mini species on tiny little lures to the biggest of our wreck predators on lures measuring up to a foot or more in length. You can spend a great deal of time, and money, choosing a range for yourself but some that I always have in my box include various Marukyu Isome worms, which I have used to catch flatfish, wrasse and even smooth-hounds, paddletails, of which shads seem to be the most popular, eels, stick lures, miniature crayfish and equally tiny crabs. To these I have added little cuttlefish and squid, tiny flatfish and a variety of other lures that, to my mind's eye, looked like they would put up a lot of movement and vibration underwater. Some of them are designed to be fished on their own, like the 12g black fiish minnow, while others need a bit of added weight or a jig head to cast them any distance.

One area of development which I am particularly thankful for is the drop shot, a style of lead weight designed for easy release from the line if it becomes snagged. Basically this is a lead weight with a specially shaped swivel embedded in it. The eye of the swivel has been flattened so that it grips the line rather than being tied to it. If your lead becomes snagged, the line will stretch when you pull for a break and the weight will drop off so that you can recover any hooked fish and the rest of your gear.

To tie the tackle is quite simple. You attach a hook above the weight with a palomar knot before mounting the lure of your choice. The diagram below will show you what to do but, in all honesty, I think that there are better alternatives. Personally I don't like the palomar knot – it can be weak and unreliable – and I don't like the fact that any fish taking the lure will brush its lips against the strands of line both above and below it.

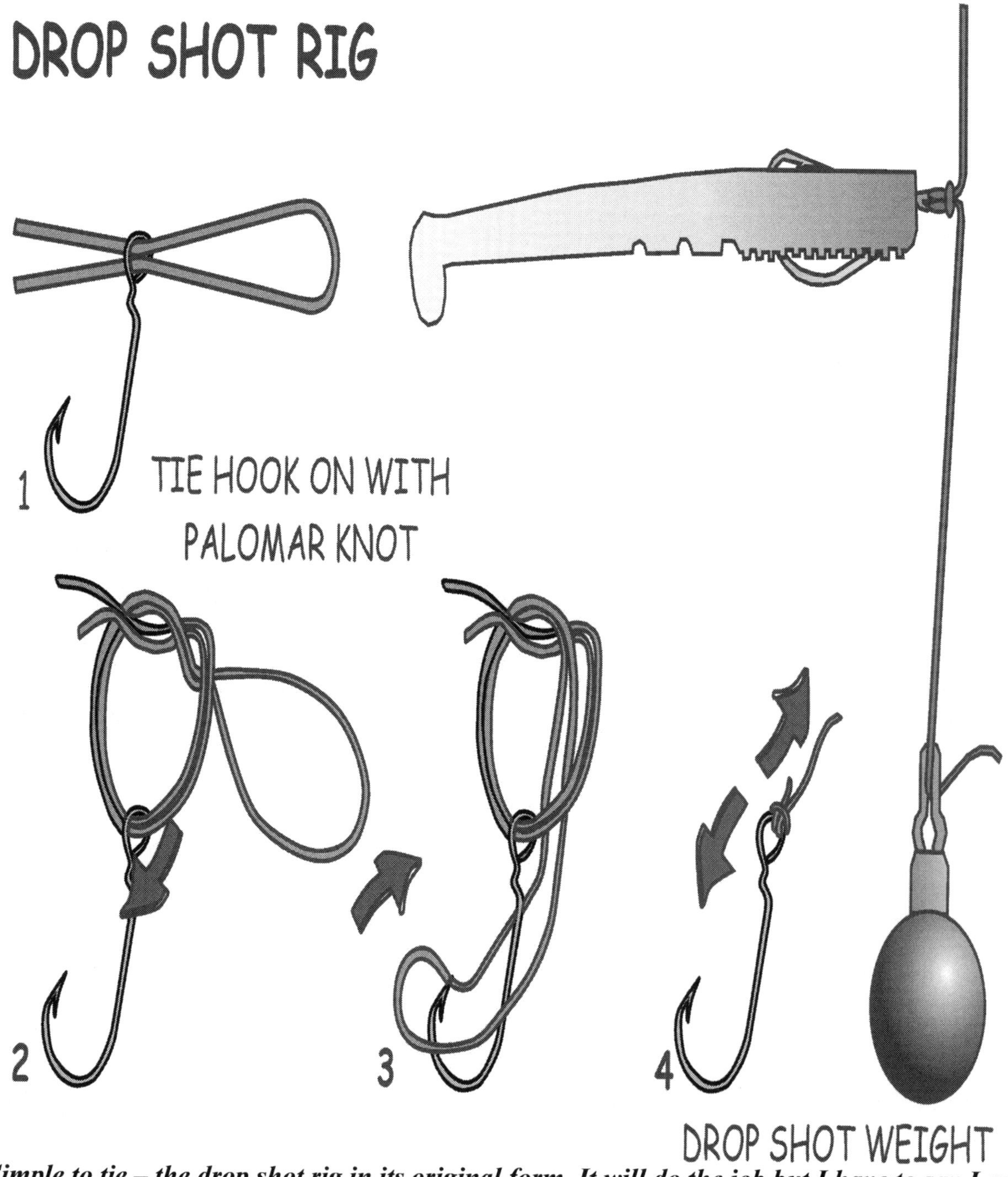

Simple to tie – the drop shot rig in its original form. It will do the job but I have to say I am not a fan.

To get rid of these niggles, I decided to make up a new tackle using a blood bight loop instead of a palomar knot. For ease of reference, I decided to call it the bight rig.

1. Take the end of your line and double it back to make a really big loop – about a foot or so long. Hold both strands of the loop together.
2. Turn it back on itself, crossing over the doubled strands.
3. Go into the middle of the loop from underneath and then over the opposite side.
4. Go back, from underneath, into the space that is left at the end. Pull the whole loop through before moistening and pulling tight.

Cut one side of the loop so that you are left with a long strand and a short strand. You can then attach the weight and the hook to please yourself.

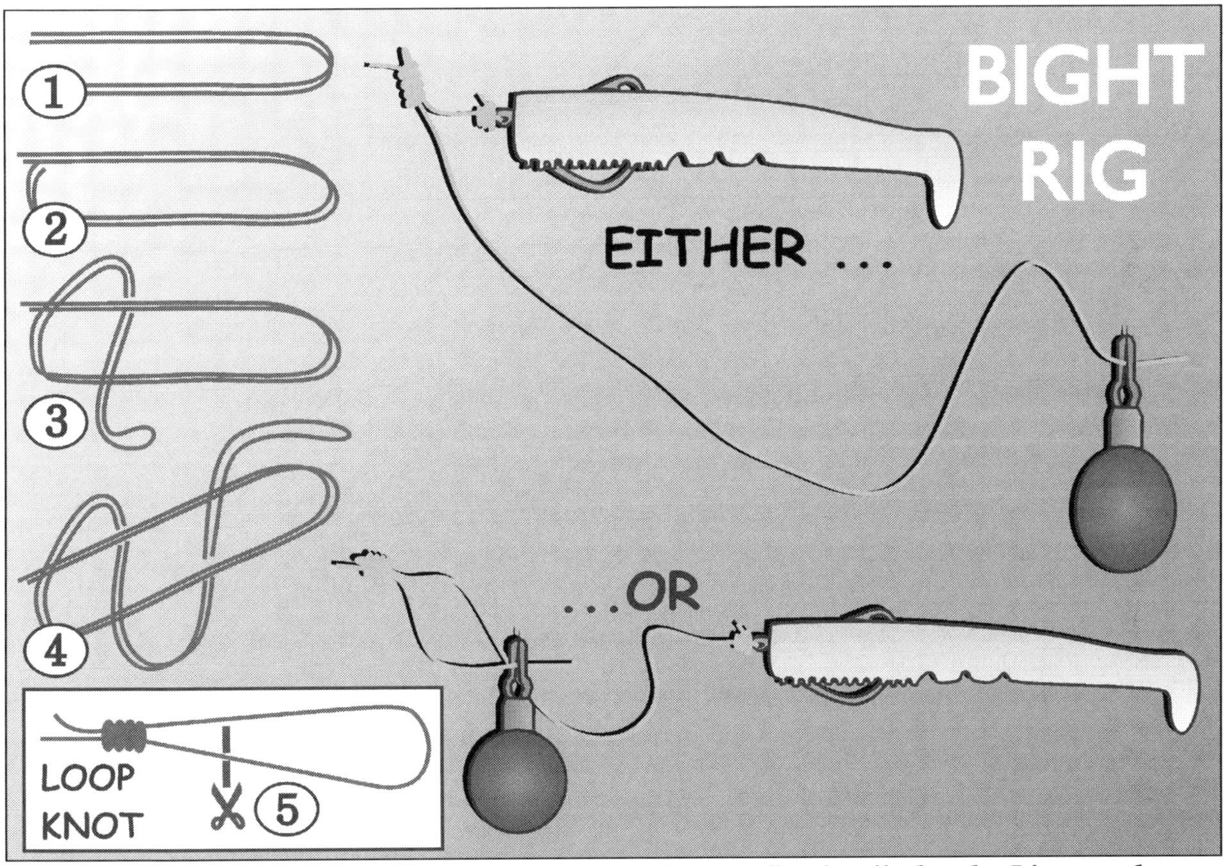

This is the tackle that I prefer. Quite often I will put a floating jig head – I import them from America – or a buoyant bead on the longer trace. This works especially well with Marukyu Isome worms.

If you put the lure in the up position, this does exactly the same as a conventional drop shot rig but, when a fish bites, its lips will not close against the upper and the lower strands of line. They are not there! Now I could be wrong but my own experience suggests that this makes the fish slightly slower to reject the lure, which gives you a slightly increased chance of hooking them. It also means that the palomar knot to the hook is replaced with a grinner knot, in which I have much more confidence.

Swapping the positions of the hook and the weight opens up some interesting possibilities, especially if you put on a floating jig head or a buoyant bead just before the hook. Any little twitch of the rod tip makes the lure rise, dart and quiver, which has got to be more interesting for the fish.

I also found that, if you used a permanent marker and drew a pair of eyes on a buoyant bead, this resulted in much more aggressive takes, especially from wrasse. Now whether or not this is appealing to their territorial instincts, I can't say for sure, but it definitely makes a difference. I also found that it had a much greater impact on red beads than on yellow or luminous beads. (I often use the latter in the dusk, keeping a UV torch handy to zap up the luminescence whenever it seems to be fading.)

Another aspect of using a buoyant bead on the longer trace is that you can experiment with tactics designed to take advantage of neutral buoyancy. I had great fun with garfish when I used a mackerel strip on this setup, matching the tackle to a drop shot weight that was only just heavy enough to slowly, very slowly, sink the bead. It really delayed the drop through the water and I had a lot of bites as a result.

Not that garfish were the only ones to attack the bait, with pollack and mackerel taking it just as readily albeit at slightly greater depths. In practice it seemed to be that the garfish were first upon the bait, followed by mackerel and then, finally, by pollack.

Of course, using bait with LRF tackle is slightly frowned upon by some 'purists' but for me, personally, I don't see the harm in it. If I am catching fish and having fun then why on Earth does it matter? Match your bait to the location and the food sources available and you can catch a lot more fish by experimenting with lures and bait (separately, not together) than you will with lures alone.

Using the buoyant beads also made me wonder what would happen if you deliberately fished the tackle in a way that would target the upper layers of water. Accordingly I tried this out in an estuary, ripping the tackle quickly through the water with real arm wrenching movements. The results were very good – I caught a lot of bass when the people around me were catching nothing at all. Then, later on in the tide, this position was reversed and they started catching while the bites that I had been having dried up. Fortunately I had a bigger drop shot lead with me and this was on the rig within seconds, when I started to catch again, albeit by letting the tackle sink to the bottom and then retrieving more slowly.

Another variation on this theme was to use a bubble float – a hollow plastic ball designed to fish on the surface. I tied the main line to one side and a four foot long trace to the other, pulling it quickly through the water with a sandeel imitation on the hook. This definitely proved popular with the bass though I can take no credit for the idea having watched another angler do this on the Isle of Wight. (My family and I noticed him in a boat as we were getting off the Southampton ferry.) It does raise other possibilities though, like replacing the float with a piece of wood shaped and painted like a popper, a type of plug designed to float on the surface and throw up little splashes of water as it is dragged in to shore. I haven't tried it yet but I will very soon. I think it will work very well, which is why I am mentioning it here. If anyone else fancies giving it a go, we could compare results.

When I use light rock fishing tackle, I like to use braid on the reel. Since the tackle is designed to sink, it does the job very well although I always attach a short length of seventeen pounds breaking strain fluorocarbon to the end of the line with a bight loop in the braid and a albright knot to connect the fluorocarbon. I then attach a length of weaker fluorocarbon to the stronger using blood bight loops and loop to loop connections. Again, this isn't standard, but it does give me the advantage of being able to prepare rigs in advance and then change them in seconds, for example if I lose a rig in the rocks. The stronger fluorocarbon virtually never breaks so I can be up and running again within seconds.

I suppose that part of my logic with this is that I find attaching thin fluorocarbon directly to braid very fiddly. It takes me longer to do this than to tie up a new rig. Having a selection of rigs and lures prepared in advance means that I lose very little fishing time, which is, after all, very precious.

If you think about it, like most of us I spend far more time working than I get to spend going fishing. It would be nice if it was the other way round but in today's pressured environment, I find my leisure time being more and more squeezed by the necessity of making a living. If using a strong link means that I can squeeze in a few extra casts then, as far as I am concerned, that is all to the good.

Of course you will need to learn how to do a loop to loop connection and one more knot – the needle knot. The first is easily taken care of with the picture below hopefully explaining the process in sufficient detail for you to take care of this on your own. You can even practice with rubber bands if you like!

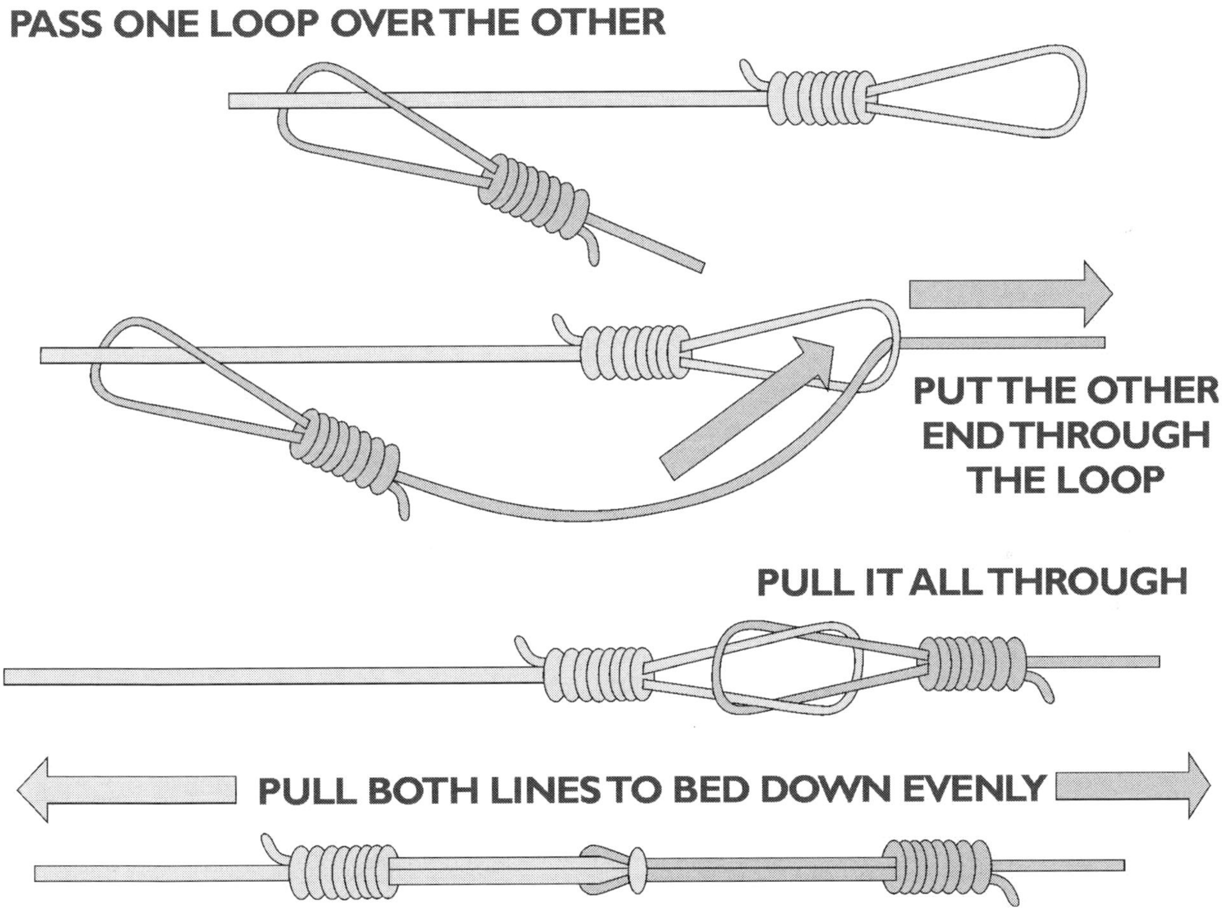

The albright knot is a bit more tricky with a lot of people using a needle – I use a cake tester - to help them tie the knot. Once you have got the hang of it, you can speed up a little but, with braid and thin lines, I still find it fiddly and easier to do in the comfort of my own home rather than down by the water's edge with breezes and glare off the water to contend with.

Let me talk you through the process and then you can make up your own mind.

1. Tie either a bimini hitch or a blood bight loop in the braid.
2. Thread the length of stronger fluorocarbon up through the loop and then lay a needle at the side.
3. Turn the end of the fluorocarbon back on itself and then, working from the back towards the front, wrap it ten or eleven times around both the loop and the needle.
4. When you get to the open bit of loop left at the front, tuck the end of the fluorocarbon through it – and this is important – the opposite way to how you started.

5. Wet it and pull tight. Sometimes I find it helpful to open the coils up a bit, going towards the braid rather than away from it, before smoothing everything down and then pulling the knot by tugging on both strands of the fluorocarbon.

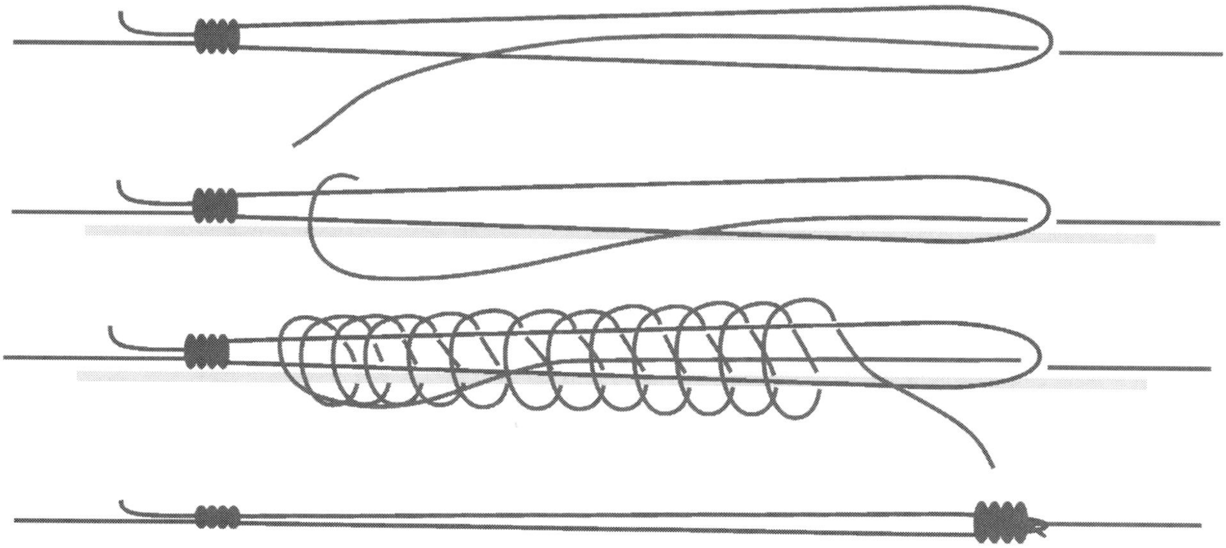

Not, I find, the easiest knot to do down at the water's edge, especially in windy conditions. I prefer to do it at home, where its strength and neatness more than justifies the investment in time.

Recently I have seen some ridiculously convoluted knots used to join nylon to braid. Out of all of the knots that I have discovered, I found this one the most manageable.

As a coach, I sometimes take parties of students fishing. On one occasion, I was leading a course on sea angling within a local secondary school. Since Sportivate, the body responsible for funding the course, was concentrating on their 'This Girl Can' campaign, I found myself strolling along the breakwater with a group of young ladies, all of them enjoying the sunshine and determined to catch.

For this particular trip, I had decided that we were going to have a go at light rock fishing using floating jig heads and Isome worms on some rods and natural bait – ragworms – on the others. Since the girls were all new to angling I wanted to outfit them with rods that were capable of doing a good job without breaking the bank, choosing Shakespeare seven foot agility rods. I matched these up with 1000 size Shimano Hyperloop fixed-spool reels and fitted them all with light braid.

By shopping around, I had been able to get the outfits for a reasonable price – about £35 for rods and reels combined if I remember correctly. Of course it helped that I was buying half a dozen or so outfits, but it always pays to shop around for fishing tackle. Some places treat recommended retail prices as fixed and inviolate, which is fine if that's what they want to do, but a lot of others are prepared to offer slightly better prices, especially in today's very competitive market. It is usually worth having a quick look around to see what's available.

If the rods broke, well, that was just one of those things. On LRF rods, the reason why they usually break is that people reel in too far, bringing the tackle up against the top ring. Since this is mounted on a fine diameter length of fibreglass, it bends but it can only bend so far. Keep reeling and it is dragged around in a complete but tiny arc to the second ring, which is more than it can take. Something has to give and what usually happens is that the top ring breaks off and the tip section splinters, rendering the rod useless.

Of course the thing to do is to simply not reel in too far, which is fine when you are experienced, but not quite so easy when you are both young and excited. Bear it in mind though and, while we're on the subject of not breaking rods, buy yourself a landing net. These rods are not designed for swinging heavy fish ashore. Put a lot of weight on a tiny tip and it will break. A landing net, especially one with soft, knotless mesh, will prevent that happening. It is also a good idea to get yourself an extending, heavy duty handle rather than an aluminium or lightweight one. Aluminium, while it looks sturdy, tends to degrade over time and will buckle when you least expect it. As for lightweight ones, well you never know what you are going to catch and, on that red letter day when something unexpectedly large turns up, do you really want to chance landing it with a flimsy handle? I certainly wouldn't, which is why I use heavy duty handles designed for big carp.

Stopping at the second set of steps, I showed the girls how I tend to fish these tackles. Casting out, I click the bale arm over at the last second so that the tackle sinks on a tight line, which is important if a fish takes on the drop. I count the tackle down until it hits bottom and then I start a slow retrieve with twitches, pauses and little pulls.

And I do mean little. I try not to move the tip of the rod more than six inches, using a quick, precise tug that dips the floating bead and then lets it flutter back up to its previous height in the water. I have often found, if I then leave this for a second or two, that fish will go for the bait with a very aggressive take.

On the day, this worked well, with a variety of wrasse and mini-species taking the hook. Some of the wrasse were sizeable, which was good, but there were a lot of small corkwing wrasse present, which tend to be very bold and very quick on the bait. They are not easily deterred either. I have seen them follow up the bait to take it right at the angler's feet, sometimes in no more than four inches of water. For the girls, when this happened, they didn't mind in the slightest. A fish was a fish and at least they had caught one.

Palm-sized ballans and little corkwing wrasse were the order of the day. This one took a floating jig head baited with a couple of small ragworms.

As the girls dispersed over the rocks, a couple of excited cries soon announced that one of them had caught a fish big enough to use the landing net. It gave some spirited runs, accompanied by some wonderful facial expressions that, for me, encapsulated what LRF is all about, which is that it can be very exciting. For me, that's one of the things that I most enjoy about teaching youngsters. Their excitement is written all over their faces, which is just wonderful to watch.

Two fascinated young anglers peer down at a ballan in the mesh. Did it really fight as hard as all that? For these two, it was also their first sight of a ballan, which are often one of the first species to respond to LRF tactics.

Over the afternoon, with the tide rising so that it hit high tide at the exact midway point of our trip, the girls continued to land a variety of species. Some tompot blennies and shannies appeared, as did gobies, but there were enough bigger fish mixed in amongst them to make things a bit more interesting.

Watching one girl, who had never caught a fish before, I saw the rod twitching over and over again. Each time she struck but was just that little bit too late. However, despite that, she didn't give up. I showed her how to cast a little bit further out and set her up on a diagonal line which would bring the tackle – a bight rig fitted with a buoyant bead and baited with ragworm - past a rocky underwater outcrop where I knew the wrasse tended to congregate.

Within seconds she had a savage bite, struck valiantly, but, unfortunately, missed it. She started to reel in to recast but I told her to let the tackle sink again and then bring it in very slowly, even though, by now, she was only about fifteen to twenty feet out. I could see, every few seconds, her rod twitch with a bite which she didn't quite manage to hook. She was getting faster and more confident but she wasn't quite there yet.

Then, seconds before she was about to take it out from the water, the tip pulled round savagely – and I do mean savagely! It caught her by surprise and nearly pulled the rod from her hands before she clutched it in a death grip and pulled back so hard the line almost sizzled through the water.

Back and forth the two struggled. The fish gained a bit of line against the drag but was then hauled closer to shore every time that it paused. Top lip caught between her teeth, the young angler - making, from time to time, I have to say, strange and rather unladylike exclamations - pulled it nearer and nearer to hand until it was time to reach for the net.

Then, much to both of our dismay, the fish spat the hook. I think it took advantage of a little bit of slack and used the opportunity to get rid of it. The two of us froze in absolute horror and, to her credit, I think only a heroic act of will stopped her from dashing the rod on the rocks. She was definitely not impressed, burying her face in her hands while I looked on, not saying anything because it wasn't quite the moment to do so. She needed a couple of minutes to get over the frustration of losing the fish at the last possible moment. It was really bad luck.

Good for her though, within minutes she was casting again and, this time, she was hooking the fish that were biting. Unfortunately they were tiny, tompot blennies, shannies and a goldsinny, but she cheered up and started to enjoy herself again. She didn't mind that the fish were small, which is the case with a growing number of LRF anglers. Many of them are quite happy to catch little fish.

Now, for me, mini species are a by catch that you can't really avoid with LRF tackle. I far prefer bigger fish, which suits my philosophy of trying to catch them on the lightest possible tackle so as to maximise the sport available. However some people really like to catch them and target them deliberately. I have even known some of them go down, at the low tide, to big rockpools at the water's edge, catching scorpion fish, gobies and a variety of blennies. That's not something that I would do, I'm afraid, it just doesn't do it for me but it's fine if that's what you enjoy.

I suppose the closest that I have come to it is when I have fished for eels in some really tiny pools, one in the middle of a car park where a drain emptied into a marshy area some twenty feet across. It was very small but it held eels weighing a couple of pounds or so, which were good fun on a bight rig fished hard on the bottom. They put up a surprising scrap, considering the surroundings, but they were also large enough to be interesting, which is why I was there in the first place. On an LRF rod, their grudge match style of fighting really put the blank through its paces, showing just how tough these little rods can be.

Naturally I ignored the occasional glances from passers-by who clearly thought that I was insane!

But I digress. My young companion, having recovered her equanimity, seemed quite content to catch the smaller fish, though I suspect that the reason she wouldn't move from the spot was in the hopes that the larger fish would return. It wouldn't of course, no doubt it was sulking somewhere in the depths, hidden in the rocks, but she was happy enough to carry on as she was so I went to check on the others.

By now every one of them had caught fish, most, I have to say, on the small side, but, all in all, it had been a good afternoon, with the girls trying really hard. They had a lot of bites, caught a good number of fish and even had some encounters with a few bigger ones. One of them, in addition to my young friend of a few moments before, had also lost a superb ballan, but she had gone on to catch a couple of medium sized fish and seemed, when I spoke to her, quite content.

It can be really frustrating to lose a good fish, especially when it is almost at your feet, but it does go to show what LRF is all about. You never know exactly what is going to take your bait but, by golly, especially in the Summer, LRF will get you the bites. Whether or not you get the fish, well that's something that will improve over time, especially as your experience grows. It's certainly well worth giving it a go and can be absolutely ideal for those just starting out. I would certainly recommend it.

Little corkwings appeared regularly through the afternoon.

Chapter Four: Flounder Fishing

Mention flounder fishing to the majority of anglers and they tend to think about bottom fishing with lots of beads and heavy weights to combat the strong tides that are so often found in the estuaries where these obliging flatfish reside. It is certainly a method that catches fish but, if we are being brutally honest, it is an approach that I find quite boring. You cast out, stick the rod in a stand and wait for the fish to hook themselves. Then, since flounders tend to be massively outgunned on the rods that are in use, they are usually dragged unceremoniously ashore with little other than a flick of their tail in protest.

Fortunately you can turn the sport on its head by using the same tackle that I have described in the previous chapters. A fish capable only of whimpers on a beachcaster is transformed beyond recognition on lighter rods such as spinning and LRF rods. They become much more interesting targets, fighting hard for their freedom and capable of turning a lack lustre day into a red letter one instead.

The key is lighter tackle. A beachcaster is designed to hurl a big lump of lead a distance from the shore. Compared to the inherent power to be found in such a blank, a small flounder has little or no chance of winning its freedom. They are not big enough. However, catch the same fish on a spinning rod designed to cast a 21g weight and, all of a sudden, you are giving it a fighting chance. Its sudden lunges and sprints will put a satisfying bend in the rod and a smile on the angler's face.

For me, I love to catch them but I tend to use methods that most other anglers ignore. I do, for example, love float fishing, especially in estuaries where there are plenty of sandeels. I don my waders, set the float to just off the bottom and drift it down with the tide, waiting until it is almost washed ashore before I finally retrieve it.

And there is method in my apparent madness. I have caught flounders less than ten feet from the shore, where they are hiding out of the grip of the current and out of the sight of their potential predators. It is no accident that paddlers are often startled by stepping on flounders that make an abrupt bolt for freedom. They are there because their camouflage makes them confident and their flattened body shape makes it easy for them to manoeuvre quickly in water too shallow for most estuary species. These are natural advantages that they exploit and which the angler, if you think about it, should also use to his or her advantage.

I do, however, like to adapt my float tackle. I used to experiment with all sorts of sizes and shapes of floats, not to mention variations in the rig itself, but now I tend to stick to the West country sliding floats capable of suspending a 21g weight. They are great and, with a bit of ingenuity, enable me to change quickly between float tackle and a leger rolling on the bottom, albeit not the stationary leger used with beachcasting tackle. All I do, when I make the wire links that I mentioned in chapter two, is to make the opposite eye to the swivel into a snap link. I then attach the main line with a blood bight loop.

To change from float to rolling leger I open the snap link, slide off the bead and float, then reattach the weight. Instant rolling leger! To change back to float I open the snap link, slide the float and bead back on and then reattach the weight. Result? Instant float! Simple to make, simple to use and, to be honest, I wish that I had thought of it years ago!

To fish the tackle, I bait with a live, or recently dead sandeel, and then wade out to just below chest height. I set the float to fish about three inches off the bottom and then cast out a short distance, allowing the current to drift the tackle down with the tide and gently towards the shore. If I get bites, I stick to float, but if I don't then I swap over to leger and feel for them instead.

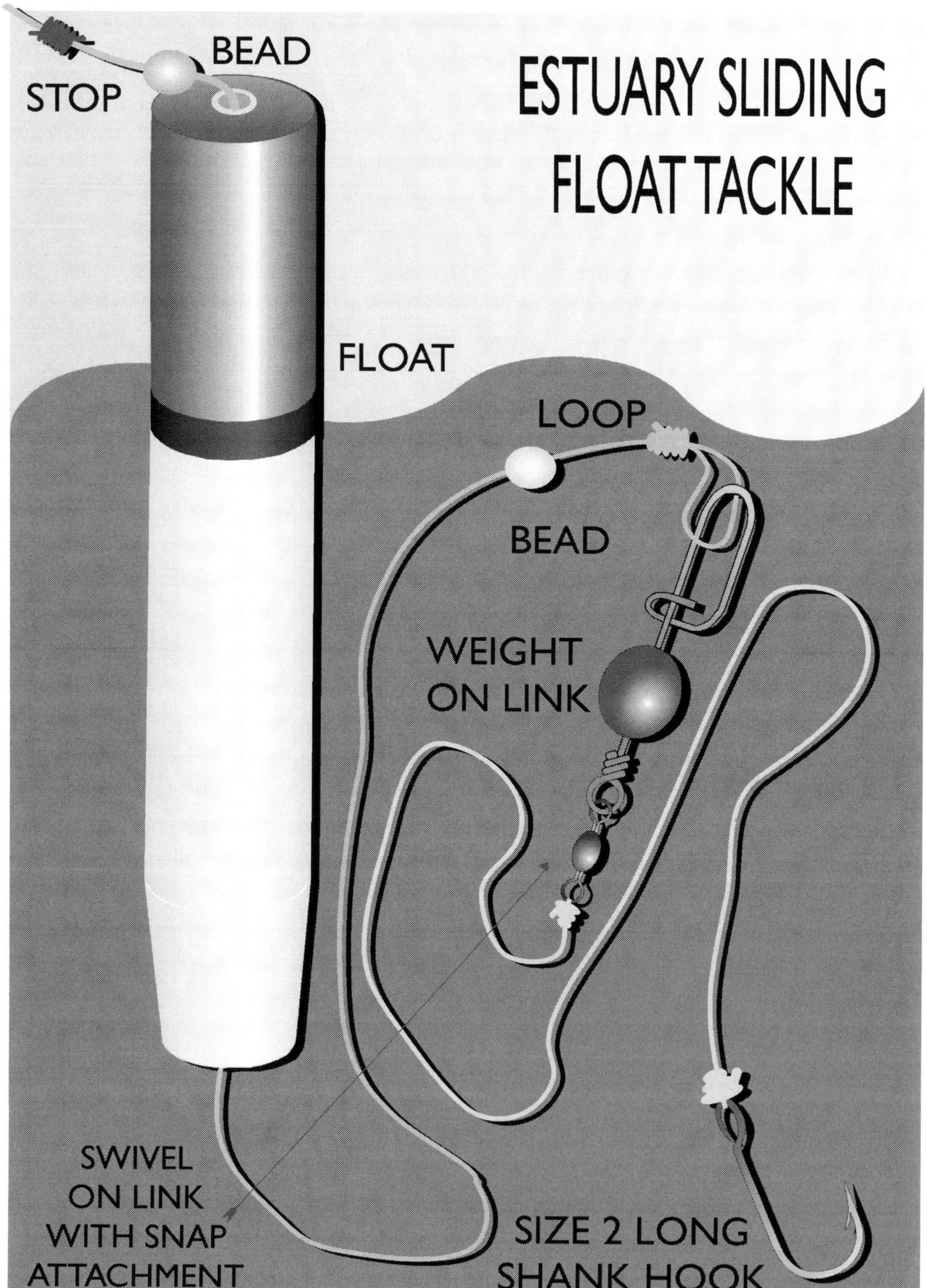

Sliding float tackle for estuaries. Almost identical to the float tackle that I use for mackerel but with a quick change facility that enables me to chop and change my tactics according to the conditions that I find on the day.

I remember, on one particular day, that I arrived too late in the tide to enjoy the bass fishing that I had been hoping to do. There had been an accident and the resulting traffic was absolutely horrendous, making me almost two hours later than I had originally planned. The tide had dropped too far for the bass, with the water too shallow, but the sandeel netters had eels and there was always the chance of a flounder. Rather than give up on the trip, I decided to go for these instead.

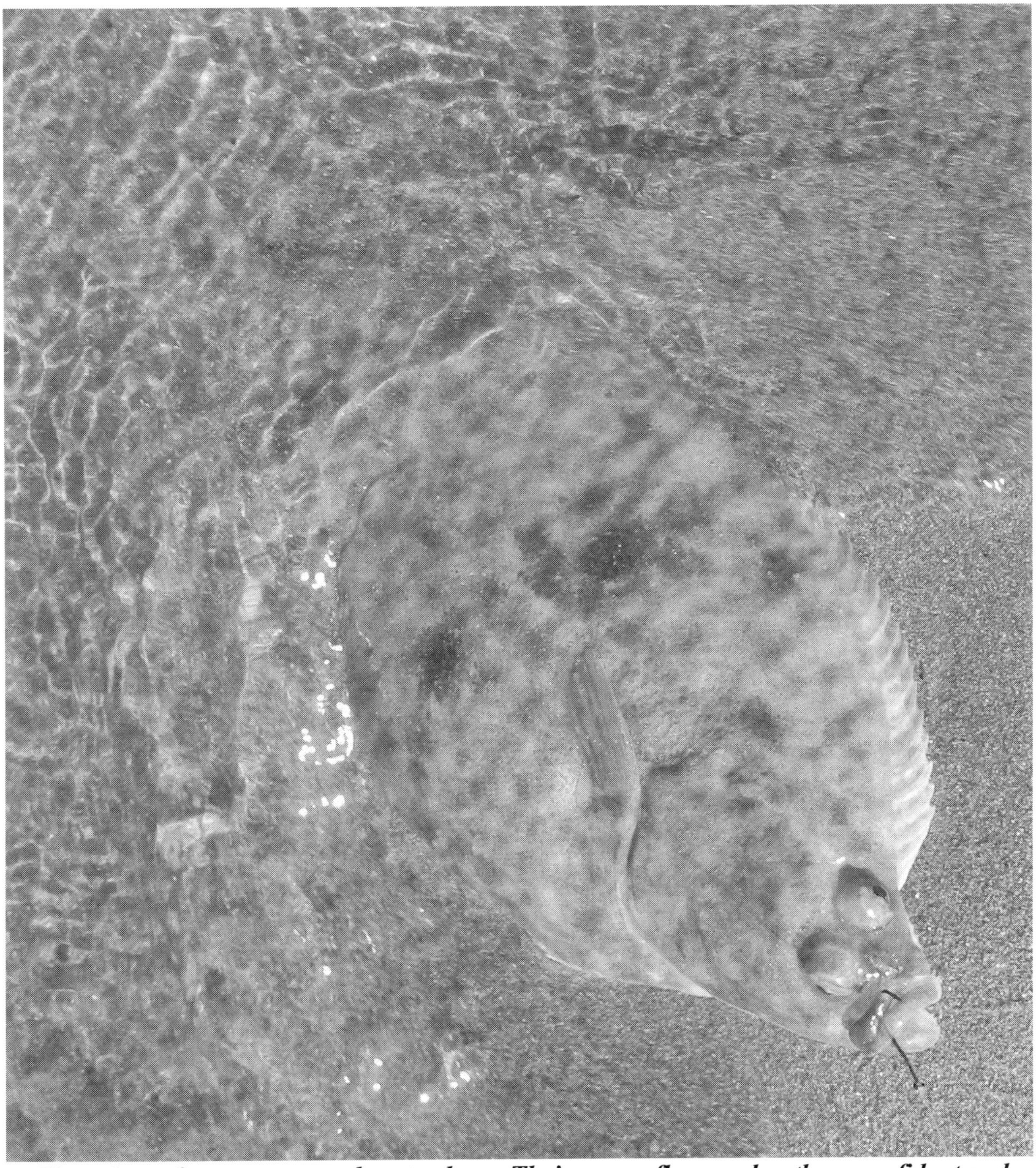

Flounders often come very close to shore. Their camouflage makes them confident and their flattened body shape makes it easy for them to manoeuvre quickly in water too shallow for most estuary species.

Slipping on my waders, I paddled out until the water was just below my chest. I set the float to just off the bottom, baited up with a small sandeel – often more attractive to flounders than great big ones – and cast my float some twenty feet from where I was standing.

For a while, I had nothing. The tide was dropping fast, the current was slowing and I was soon at waist, rather than chest, height. The float was barely moving and, on a whim, I let it drag itself almost to the shore, no more than ten feet from the water's edge. It was so shallow that the float lay listlessly on its side but then, with an abrupt movement, it slipped under the surface and away. I tightened up, letting the fish hook itself against the bend in the rod, and felt the light spinning rod that I was using come alive as the flounder made a spirited dash to try and get away.

I had some fun playing it in but it wasn't a big one and was soon nestling in the folds of my landing net. I unhooked it, posed for a couple of photographs and then let it swim safely off, presumably, if it had any sense, looking for pastures new.

Not big but great fun on light tackle!

Before I baited up again, I decided to change to leger. The tide had slowed almost to nothing, which I have personally found is often a very good time for sport with estuary flounders, but the bullet lead would still have a bit of movement. Now I like that, figuring that a sandeel able to move slightly but otherwise fairly helpless, would appeal to the flounders' predatory nature. In the past, I have had some very good sport with this approach so I saw no reason to question it now.

Drifting the tackle down with the tide, I caught a couple of medium-sized flounders which put a good bend in the rod that I was using. Then the bites dried up so I decided to move upstream a little.

I had been fishing just down from where the sandeel netters placed their courges – wooden boxes with holes drilled in them in which they store the sandeels before selling them to the public. My reasoning for this is that sometimes, well quite often actually, the smaller sandeels tend to escape through the holes in the boxes. However, by the time they manage this, they are usually exhausted and are caught by the current, getting swept downstream. The flounders in the area soon wise up to this and a few of them station themselves where they can take advantage of this free bounty. These are the ones that I had been targeting.

Now, with the easy pickings, so to speak, cleaned up, I needed to move elsewhere so I changed back to float, waded upstream and into slightly deeper water, and proceeded to try my luck there.

One tip that it is worth pointing out here is to keep a bit of nylon in your pocket for when you want to change back to float. You can then thread it through the float, through the loop on the end of the tackle and back through the float again. It makes it much easier to pull the loop through the float, which can be a bit fiddly otherwise. You can even do the same thing for the bead, giving it a hard jerk if you need to.

For a while nothing happened but then, slowly, the float was inexorably pulled underwater. It was too slow for a bass, too quick for a crab, so I gave it a second and then swept the rod round into a very satisfying curve.

The fish at the other end pulled back immediately, surprising me with just how strong it was. It got its head down and then tried to kite away from me, taking line from the drag with the sound that I always like to hear. As far as I am concerned, it's always a good day when a fish is strong enough to take line against the drag.

Talking of which, when you are using light tackle, it's always worth taking a few moments to set the drag to the correct tension. Too loose and it will spin and could even cause a bird's nest, a massive tangle of line. Too tight and you could break your trace or pull the hook from the fish's mouth. You want it so that the fish can take line but it has to be against pressure, making sure that it has to work for it.

Catch a flounder on a beachcaster and the fight is dictated by how fast you can wind it in. That's not the case with light tackle. The struggle that this fish was giving was out of all proportion to any flounder that I had ever caught before. It was a seriously big fish and, when I finally caught sight of it, I knew that it was going to be the biggest flounder that I had ever caught. I have had them well over three pounds in weight, which is a cracking size for a flounder, but they were tiddlers compared to this.

And then, disaster! A boat angler, deciding that he couldn't wait for me to finish playing the fish, if he even gave it any thought at all, gunned his engine and drove boat and engine straight over the top of my line, coming in so fast and so close that his wash almost knocked me from my feet and cut my line in half. Then, completely oblivious to the consequences of his utterly inconsiderate behaviour, in fact ignoring me altogether, he jumped out of the boat to get his eels.

If I had been standing next to the sandeels, I would have put it down to experience and probably my own fault. Thing is, I was nowhere near them. I was just in front of the bit of beach that he decided that he was going to use. I could have said something of course but to be honest just didn't see the point. I don't like arguments. They don't enrich my life and, in my opinion, very rarely achieve anything positive at all. I chalked it down to yet another encounter with an individual whose shoe size matched his IQ and retackled. I felt a bit despondent but, when you get moments like this, you just need to give yourself a little shake and try to put it out of your mind.

So I did, though, to be honest, I probably muttered under my breath for a minute or two. (I'm not a saint!) However, with tide and current at their lowest point, I decided to give something else a go.

I had brought an LRF rod with me in the somewhat forlorn expectation that I might be able to give it a try at low water. I thought that I could put on a jig head and an Isome or other soft plastic worm in the vague hope that I might get a flounder to take. It's a method that I like experimenting with but it's not a great one for the Teign, which is where I was fishing.

It's just one of those things. Virtually all of the flounders that I have caught in the Teign come up on sandeels in the summer or peeler crabs in the autumn and winter. I have never had much luck with ragworms, at least not there though I have in the Dart and other rivers. If real worms didn't work terribly well then it didn't give me a lot of confidence in an imitation worm but then, I figured, you would never know unless you tried. Accordingly I put on a 3g jig head and a curly tailed worm and gave it a go.

Without, I have to say, any success on this occasion though it is a tactic worth bearing in mind. On some rivers, especially a little way from the coast, it can be really successful, but the Teign doesn't appear to be one of them.

However, since I enjoyed using the LRF rod, I decided to give another strategy a try, making up a bight rig, albeit in this case without a floating bead and a slightly larger hook. I baited this with a small live sandeel and then popped the 8g drop shot out into what little current was left.

Now normally the tide at the Teign is so strong that this would have been whisked away very quickly and I would have gone back to the float or rolling leger tackle on my spinning rod. Today, with the tide so sluggish, I got away with it, keeping lightly in contact with the tackle as it worked its way slowly downstream.

And then I picked up a flounder, not a big one but putting up an extraordinary fight on the light tackle that I was using. These rods are so light that they magnify every flurry and twitch that the fish make when they struggle against being brought to shore. However, at the same time, the power from the lower section of the blank is more than enough to deal with these and even larger fish. It was good fun, especially when this one was followed by another that was very similar in size.

The feeling of the fight on a light tackle rod is so different from conventional tackle that it bears almost no resemblance. I know I keep saying it but catch a flounder on a beachcaster and there isn't really much of a fight to speak of. The flounders are unlikely to be big enough to put up much of a struggle. You get some, especially when they are being forced off the bottom or they see the shoreline, when they try to dash away, but it is not much.

Catch the same fish on a light spinning or LRF rod and it is a totally different ball game. There is a much better match between the size of the fish and the power within the blank so that you get a real sporting encounter which, to me, is not only part of the difference between fishing and angling but really shows up why sea fishing with lighter tackle rocks. Why not try it and see?

No problem on a beachcaster but catch flounders on a much lighter rod and you will find that they can put up a really interesting fight!

A crisp Winter's day after a period of stormy weather is often a good time for fishing.

I like beachcasting, especially when the fish are plentiful, but it can be very hit or miss. Once you have used what clues there are to pick your spot, you can experiment with different tackles and baits but there is never going to be any kind of guarantee that you are going to catch. Sometimes it can just be hard! However, on occasion, a move of just a few yards can put your tackle in the midst of a shoal, which is why I like to stay easily mobile. I rarely bother with setting up a camp with a beach shelter and the like because, if the fish don't appear when I expect them to, then I prefer to try a different spot.

Sometimes you can be lucky and a short walk will put you in amongst the fish but, at other times, you might find yourself traipsing the length of the beach! It all depends on the day and the conditions.

It can also burn off a lot of calories. Walking can be absolutely fine on hard packed sand but just try it on shifting shingle and grit or loose blow away sand where your feet sink inches into the beach's surface with every step that you take. Even a walk of a few hundred yards takes its toll, which is why I like to give myself every advantage that I possibly can, not the least of which is making sure that I am wearing warm, breathable clothing, building up base layers beneath a wind and waterproof jacket or suit.

I also like to tackle up before I go so that I can make the most of the time at my disposal. However it can be a little awkward to carry rods that are already assembled with terminal tackle and weights at the ready so, after one particularly frustrating trip, I decided that I would turn my tripod into a carrying device rather than just being a rest to lean my rods against. That would increase my fishing time, with the rods able to get into the water more quickly, and hopefully make carting two beachcasters about a lot easier to manage. It would also be a lot more comfortable on the hands, especially on cold evenings when I had, yet again, forgotten my gloves! (Icy cold metal on flesh is never a great combination!)

I didn't want to spend a fortune though and, when push came to shove, I found that I was able to make most of the changes from bits and pieces that I had left over from previous DIY projects. The only thing that I needed to spend extra on was some thermoplastic polymorph, which I will go into more detail on shortly.

Basically, I needed two pieces of metal that I could use as arms, some wide plastic tubing, two end caps for that same tubing, some webbing, two Velcro straps, two eye bolts, two slightly longer nuts and bolts and six smaller nuts, bolts and washers.

I cut the tubing into four pieces and used these to make the holders on the end of the arms. I knew that I would have to slide the rods in and out of them so, while the bottom tubing could be left uncut, the top two pieces of tubing would need slices removed from top to bottom. I bolted these to a metal arm and then used one of the longer bolts to bolt that to the tripod about three inches down from the existing arm. I rotated the rest so that the original cups were facing upwards and then secured the new piece with the plastic holders facing down below the central portion of the tripod. That way the rods would hang downwards without getting in the way.

When I use the tripod as a rod carrier, I put a Velcro strap around both cups to stop the rods from falling out. You can see them on the first photograph in this chapter.

I made and attached the bottom arm in a similar manner only this time I used two bolts on each cup to secure the end caps, which would stop the rods from sliding through. As I said before, no slices were necessary because I wanted the rod butts to sit in these without a lot of fuss and bother. Of course you do need to make sure that the plastic tubing has a big enough diameter for this to happen, preferably before you cut it to pieces!

My final job was to make the unit easy to carry, which I decided to do with a comfortable handle sliding on a strong webbing strap, which is why I bought the polymorph.

As its name suggests, thermoplastic polymorph is a plastic material which can be heated – in this case with very hot water – and then moulded into whatever shape you want it to take. All I did was to roll it into a hollow tube and then built up the ends to stop it sliding through my hands. I then threaded the webbing though the handle and tied it to the eyes on the two eye bolts. I drilled two holes in the rest and then, making sure that the webbing didn't sag too much but was out of the way of any other fittings on the tripod – in this case the back of the middle cup - used the eye bolts to secure the webbing strap to the tripod.

The point behind the sliding handle is that I have got lots of different rods, some longer than others, so no single point would be perfect for every combination of tackle that I was going to put in the holders. This way, I could simply slip the handle up and down until I found the perfect point of balance to make carrying it easy.

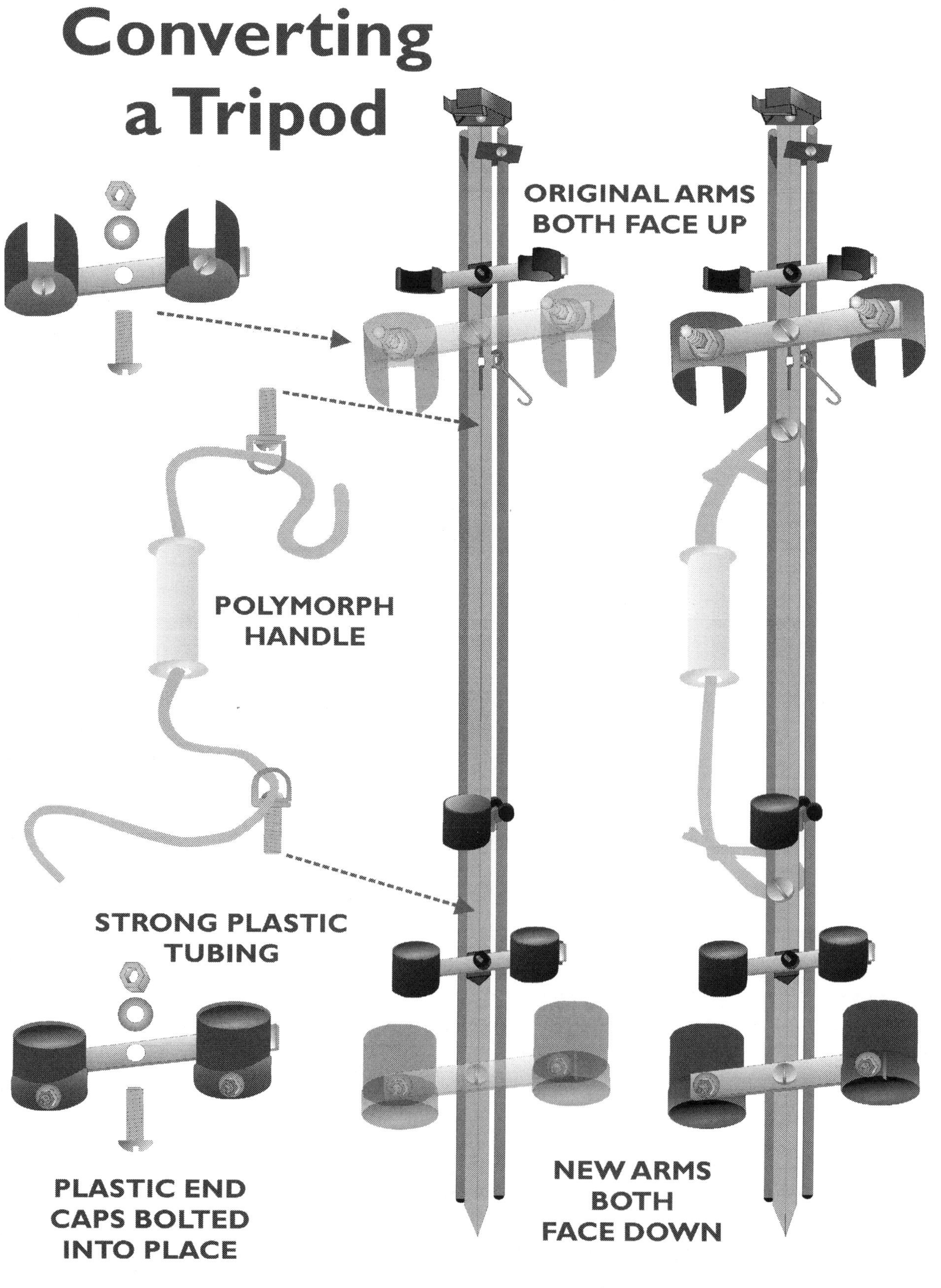

Hopefully the diagram will make the process clear but I would venture one word of caution. You need to make sure that the tripod that you are going to convert is made of sufficiently robust materials to support the whole process. There are some flimsy tripods around that might very well buckle, fold and even break and I wouldn't want that to happen. It's the central support that needs to be strong, just like the one that I have illustrated.

As I have already mentioned, I have got several different rods. If I am after big fish, I have got some heavier duty blanks while, for areas where you can get away with five ounce lead weights, I have got a couple of continental beachcasters.

For those spots where the tide and currents are minimal, I have got a pair of ultra-light beachcasters capable of putting a three ounce lead weight well over a hundred yards from the shore. These are an absolute delight to use, where you can feel every flick and dive of even the smallest of fish. I have pulled in six ounce whiting where the rod has quivered and bent strongly over with even their little lunges. Get a bigger fish on them, or stronger species like bream, and they are wonderful, transforming the sport into almost epic proportions. They are by far my favourite rods to use.

On the majority of beachcasters, whiting barely register as anything other than a little bit of weight. That's not the case when you are using lighter tackle, when you can feel even smaller fish pulling as hard as they can for the bottom

Of course it would be nice if you could get hold of them more easily but, sadly, that doesn't appear to be the case. Mine came from Portugal since the anglers over there use them far more frequently than we do over here. We just seem to be in the habit of using tackle that, in the majority of cases, is heavier than we actually need. It is such a shame since, as I have said before, they transform the fight from just about everything that you are likely to catch, at least where you don't have to contend with big tides and strong currents.

And, for those who are sceptical, I once saw an eleven year old girl pull up a fifteen pounds bull huss on a one and a quarter pounds test curve carp rod. For that matter, I have routinely had fifteen and sixteen pounds carp on a seven weight fly rod, which is lighter by far than even the rod used by that particular young lady.

The thing with a lot of sea anglers is that they just don't know how to play fish. I once took a very experienced sea angler with me to a trout lake. He hooked into a trout that I reckon was about five pounds in weight and it almost contemptuously snapped him off.

The reason this happened was that he tried to treat it the same way that he treated fish caught on a beachcaster. It was hooked so his first and only strategy was to point the rod up and reel the little devil in. Well the trout was having none of that. It shot off and snapped the line when he held it tight instead of letting it run, using the drag and pressure to tire the fish rather than brute force and ignorance! The thing is, on light tackle you get to experience far better fights than you will on conventional gear so you are going to have to play the fish properly. You can't bully them, which is what most sea anglers do. Use a lighter rod and you really get a chance to see what fish are capable of doing. The tackle is simply a much better match to their size and weight.

As long as you are sensible of course! Such beachcasters are great for fish weighing up to five or six pounds in weight, perhaps a little more, but I wouldn't go cod fishing with them. That's a totally different ball game! You have to think about where you are fishing, the species to be had and how you are going to fish for them.

I remember, on one particular day, that I was taking a young lad onto the beach for his first ever time of fishing with a beachcaster. He was only eleven, so distance was limited, and conditions weren't great – a bright, cold Winter morning – where the only real thing that we had going for us was that it was just after a couple of days of stormy weather. Now normally I would fish that mark in the evening, when there would be a few bigger fish around, but that wasn't possible today and he wanted to try his new rod out, which was fair enough.

Since he would be fishing at fairly close range, I decided to go a bit further out. The currents can be quite strong at this mark, so I decided to have a go with my five ounce continentals rather than my very light rods. They were still nice and responsive but would be better for the conditions that we faced.

Given that it was winter and particularly bright, I walked along the beach until we came to an area where the seabed drops rapidly off into deeper water. There was plenty of flotsam washed up on the beach so my decision to fish here was based upon the fact that, after the storm, this deeper water would probably be a holding ground for food scoured out and deposited by the waves. It was also close enough to some scattered rocky areas to give us the chance of something different.

I had brought along a variety of baits, with peeler crabs, ragworms, mackerel strip and squid. This gave us a few options for experimentation though my own feeling was that, if we did catch fish, they were likely to be whiting. Still the peeler crabs might tempt a bass, even this late in the season, and there might be some flatfish around so I decided to start with the worms and the crabs. I put my young companion, who was using a twelve foot light beachcaster capable of casting up to six ounces, on mackerel strip, figuring that he would be happier catching whiting rather than nothing at all.

For myself, my continental beachcasters are just over fifteen foot long and designed to be used with a fixed-spool reel that is loaded with braid. They cast long distances with a smooth application of power and I don't have to worry about high power casts such as pendulum casts. If your casting style is good, they will cast ample distance to put you amongst the fish.

I used to regularly cast pendulum style but, following major surgery, can no longer twist as easily and as quickly as I used to. My continentals let me reach almost as far as I could with my tournament rods but have the added bonus of being much lighter and more responsive to the fish that I catch. If you want to cast a long way effortlessly and you also want a good fishing tool, I would seriously recommend them.

One thing that you do have to watch out for is how you connect your leader to the braid. Now I normally tie my leader – a length of stronger line designed to take the shock of casting – straight to my main line. Since I normally cast with 5 ounce lead weights, I use 60 lbs breaking strain clear monofilament. Basically, to be safe, you use the formula 10 lbs breaking strain for each ounce of lead plus a further safety margin of 10 lbs added on to the total. This gives you 50 lbs breaking strain for 4 ounces, 60 lbs breaking strain for 5 ounce leads, 70 lbs breaking strain for 6 ounce leads, etc.

Easy enough but, when I first tried this with braid, I snapped off almost every cast. The leader would go through the rings fine at first but then snap at the point where the braid was joined to the leader. It was completely unreliable.

To solve the problem, I found that there were two possible solutions. The first was to join the braid to a tapered leader using a blood bight loop and an Albright knot, as illustrated in Chapter Three, and the second was to tie the braid to a twenty foot length of 18 lbs breaking strain line (using the same knot) and then use this to attach the leader with the tournament shock leader knot. Both methods work fine though the second is a lot cheaper.

To tie the shock leader knot, you start by wrapping the shock leader twice around your finger. Slip the loops off and pass the end of the line through the middle of both. Tease one through the other and pull into the shape of a figure of eight. Next take the thinner line and thread it, from back to front, through both eyes of the figure of eight. Twist it six times around the leader and turn it back on itself. Pass it through the first twist next to the figure of eight and then go back through and out of the figure of eight knot the same way that you went in.

The diagram should help but, basically, when you pull the knot tight you should find that the thinner line coils neatly around the leader with the ends of both lines on the other side of the figure of eight knot. It presents as a nice tapered shape that should travel through the rod rings nicely on the cast.

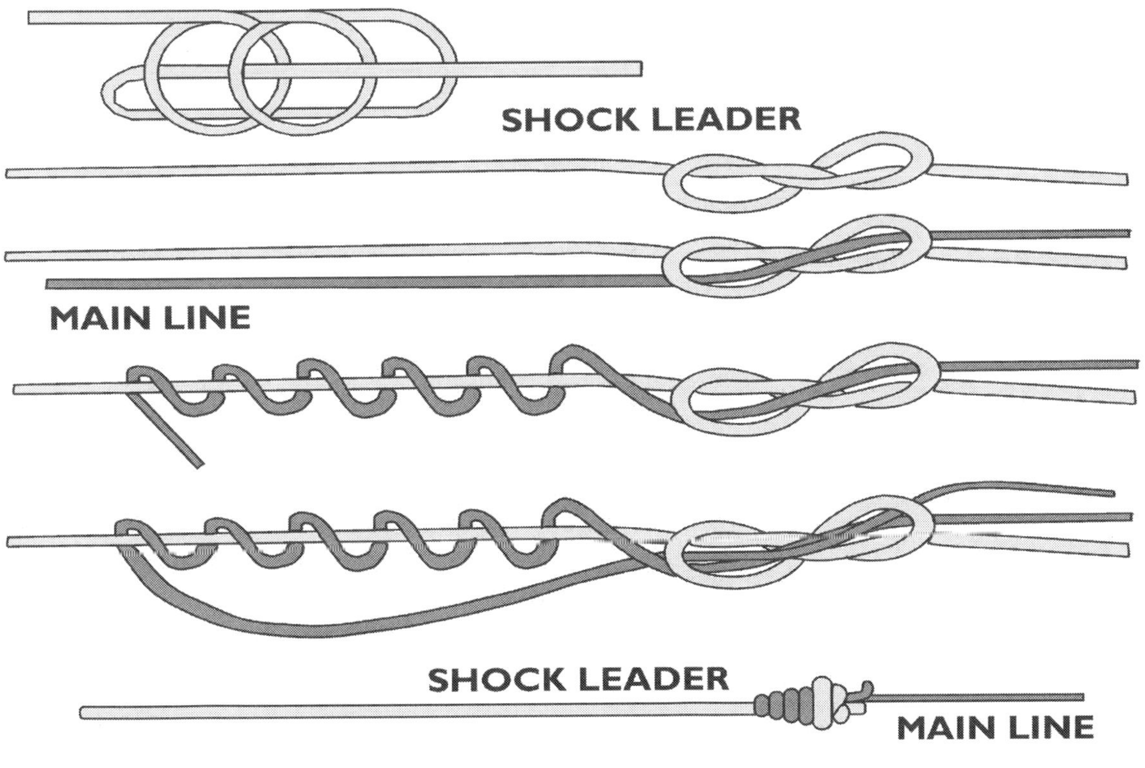

Because of his age and size, my companion was going to get on better with a four ounce weight than a five but I still put him on a 60 lbs leader. That way, if the tide should prove too strong for his tackle and start dragging it along the beach, then I could put him on a five. I knew that would keep his tackle in place even if did make casting a little bit more difficult for him.

The next decision was what tackle to put on. With a single rod, it would be better to fish with two hooks so I put him on a knotless paternoster, a simple rig which works well and is easy to tie.

Basically it is what we call a scratching rig. It presents the baits well, rarely tangles and uses swivels that spin with the short traces rather than twist them into useless spirals inside of a half dozen casts.

To make the tackle, I use Breakaway swivel tees, beads and tubing. Pass your rig line through the top of the swivel tee and out of the middle. Thread it through a bead, short length of tubing and another bead before sliding on a swivel. Turn the line back on itself and go back through both beads, the tubing and the bottom half of the swivel tee. Pull tight and then tie on a trace for the hook. Do the same again for the second hook and then tie on a link at the bottom of the rig body line ready for the weight.

KNOTLESS PATERNOSTER

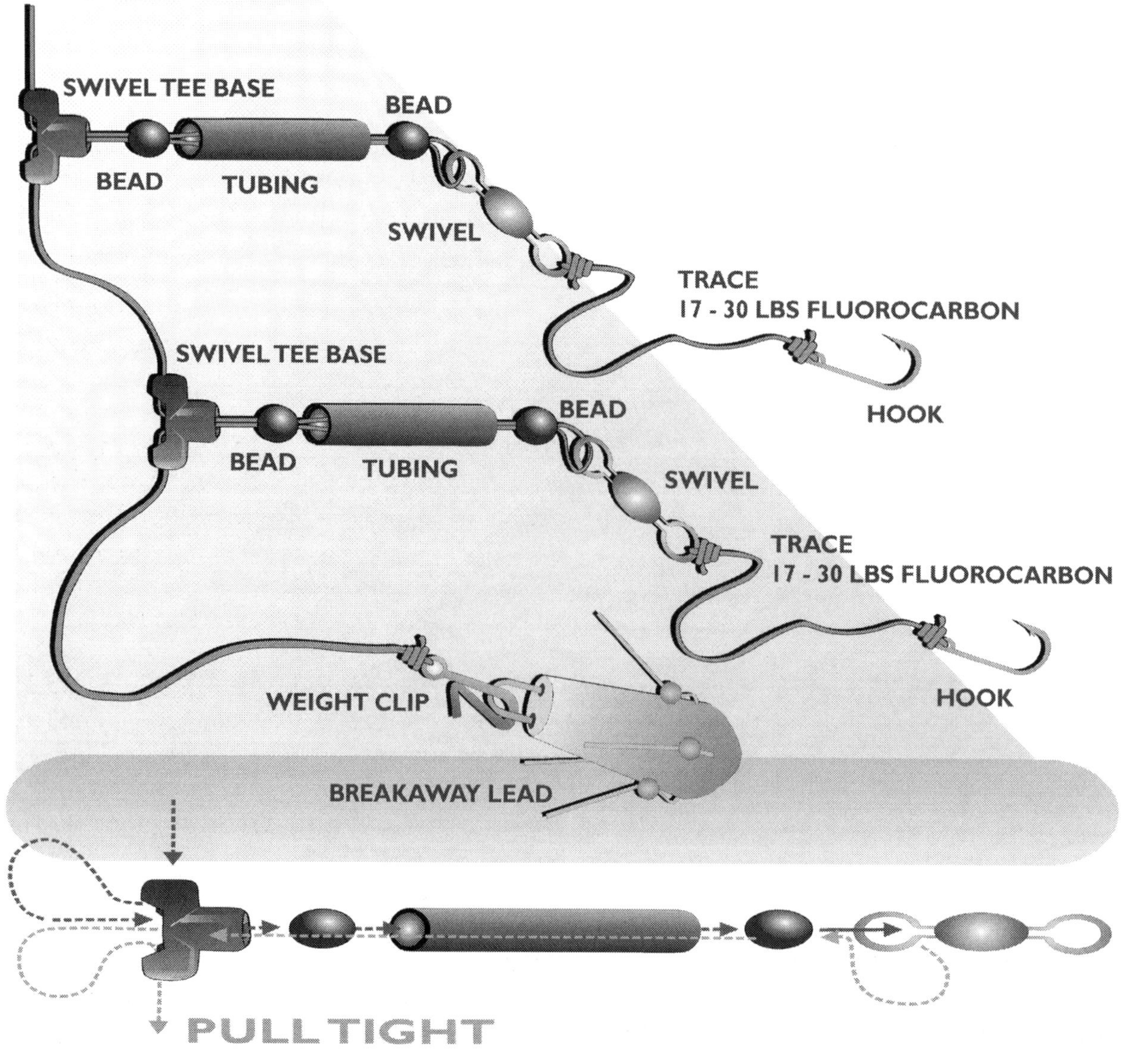

With the conditions as they were, I figured that he would be better having a go with mackerel strip for the whiting, putting a reasonably sized strip on both hooks. I hooked these three times, threading the strip along the shank until it slipped over the eye of the hook and sat on the trace above the grinner knot. I knew that this would act as a stop, thereby helping to keep the strip straight and nicely presented.

For myself, I decided to use running leger with bigger bait on one rod and ragworms on a smaller hook on the other. After the storm there was a chance of bigger fish, albeit a fairly slim chance at this time of the year and the day, but you never know so it was worth a try.

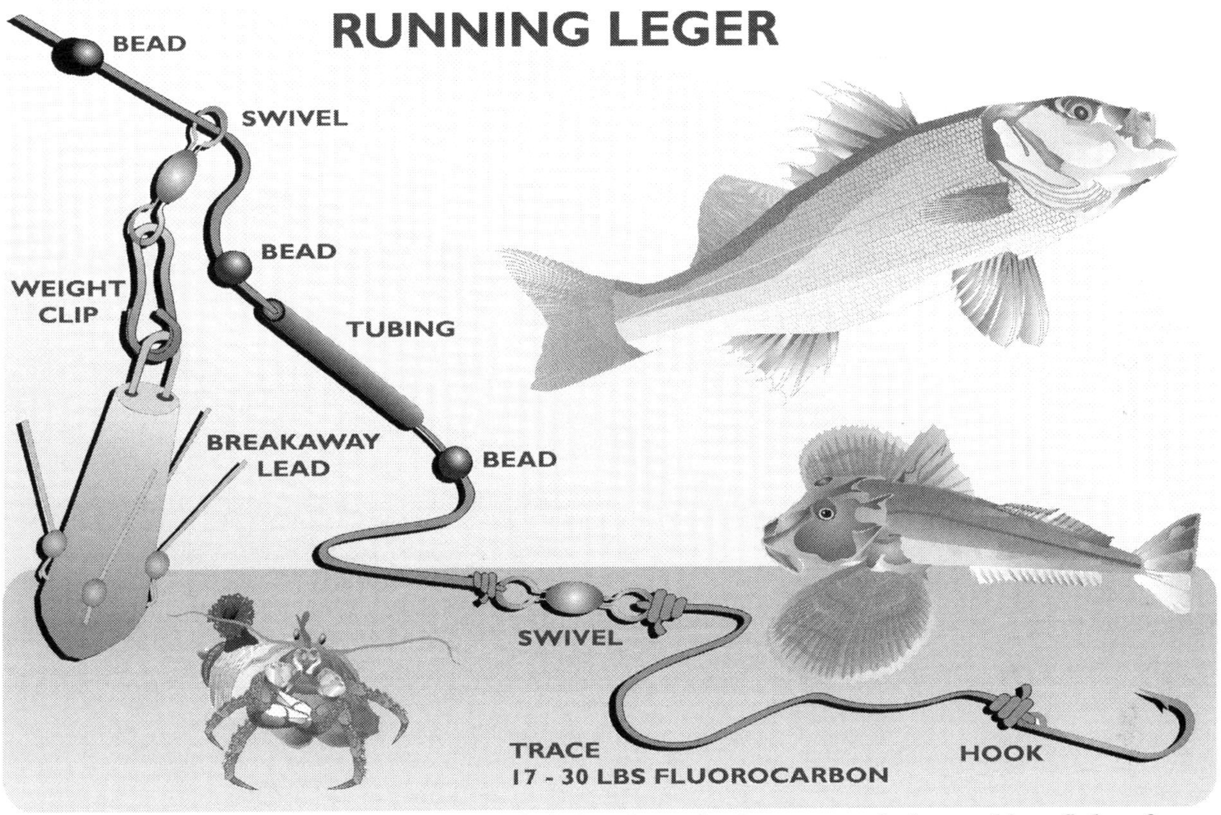

Running leger tackle presents your bait hard on the bottom and gives taking fish a few extra seconds before they feel the weight of the lead. It is a good tackle for larger fish and can also be very effective for flatfish.

So much for theory. Casting out we didn't have long to wait for the first fish with my young companion elated at a double hit of whiting, which set the scene for the rest of the morning. In the end it didn't seem to matter what bait we put on with one notable exception. The peeler crabs, which are normally a brilliant bait for sorting out the better fish, never had a take, producing absolutely no interest. Ragworms, mackerel strip and squid all scored with the whiting but the peelers, despite the fact that they were really good ones, were ignored.

If the tide had been in the evening, we would probably, at the very least at this particular mark, have had a few dogfish but, as it was, we were limited to the time we could go and how long we could stay. However, as it was his first ever trip from a beach, my young friend was quite happy with catching a few whiting and started to get better at casting, which is something that will develop as he becomes more familiar with both the tackle and the techniques involved. It gave him an easy introduction to fishing from a beach but it also showed him some simple strategies that could, under the right conditions, just as easily have produced a much wider variety of species. In the Summer, for example, assuming no hordes of eager swimmers, we could have picked up gurnard, bream, red mullet, flatfish, golden grey mullet, wrasse and pollack, to name but a few. You just never know until the day which, at least, has the charm of keeping everything fresh and interesting.

Lucky captor with a 10lbs 8ozs smooth-hound

For many people that take up fishing, the idea of a boat trip soon takes hold. It has a particular appeal - miles from shore, away from noise, work and distractions with the added bonus of a realistic opportunity for catching a big fish. No worries over the boss and pressing deadlines, just you and your tackle disappearing beneath the waves where anything could be lurking, perhaps something large, something predatory and hopefully eager to seize hold of your bait. There is something almost primal about it.

And, fortunately for us, the harbours of our varied coastline are well served by a fleet of charter boats, even though, in recent times, some of them are finding it pretty hard to keep going. When money is tight, luxury services are often the first to suffer, especially when their target audience is people like you and I, ordinary members of the public rather than the wealthy. If we are feeling the pinch in our pockets, we are less inclined to spend, which limits the number of trips that we are likely to go on.

Personally, I love getting afloat but, even though I have my own small RIB (rigid inflatable) and can, theoretically, go out whenever time and the weather allows, I still go out on several charter boats every year, making it a point to go on one, perhaps two, whenever I am on holiday. That way I can experience a variety of marks and species so that, for me at least, fishing becomes a rich tapestry of delights rather than a monotonous routine of same old, same old...

And, if there is one thing that helps me to enjoy this varied style of fishing, it is the use of light tackle. I can't even begin to tell you how many times I have seen anglers turn up with stiff, heavy rods, which they then use to catch smaller fish that they barely know are hooked. 'Well,' they often complain, 'it didn't fight much,' which is hardly surprising. If you put it in human terms it is the difference between a one on one tug of war or one against a full team of sturdy international rugby players. You can be as frisky as you like with the first but the second will see you face planted in the dirt and towed along with absolutely no control over your movements and no real chance to fight back at all!

For myself, playing fish on much lighter tackle, I never have to make this complaint. The tackle that I use so completely transforms every encounter that those same anglers often double check to see whether or not I am catching the same type of fish that they are.

I remember one trip, when we were heading out after plaice, where things did not go quite as planned. It was a beautiful day with plenty of sun but, unfortunately, after a couple of hours of unproductive drifting, the wind began to pick up, causing not only a much increased swell but also for two or three of the anglers on board to go a bit green about the gills.

Now there is not much fun in suffering from sea sickness, despite the old jokes about there being two stages to it; the first where you are afraid that you are going to die, the second where you are afraid that you are not! It can ruin a trip completely for the unfortunates concerned. However, I think that it is very possible that there is a mental component to it that isn't fully accounted for.

When I started boat fishing, I used to get seasick so I took precautions. Obviously I took the pills but I also bought some 'Sea-Bands', which were advertised as 'Acupressure Wrist Bands'. The idea was that these pushed a plastic button firmly into a pressure point that would inhibit motion sickness. Most of the time these precautions worked fine but, occasionally, I still suffered until, one day, I decided that I really enjoyed boat fishing and that there was no way that sea sickness was going to spoil my enjoyment of the day.

Now when you are suffering, people often tell you to look at the land, if you're close to it, or the horizon and concentrate on the apparent stillness of either to help to settle your symptoms. However on that particular day I decided that, come what may, I was going to completely ignore such advice. My reasoning was that people, by brooding on seasickness before, and during, a trip, actually caused it to turn into a self-fulfilling prophecy. For myself, I decided that I was going to completely ignore it. I was going to put it out of my mind because I was not going to have my fishing trips ruined. Instead I was going to give my undivided attention to the fishing itself.

And that was it. I have never been seasick since and I have gone afloat on days that would have caused me considerable discomfort before. I have had no further problems, even when people have been in the worst throes of it at my side and indeed, on several occasions, all around. Now whether or not that it is going to work for anyone else, I don't know but I do think that there is a very good chance that it will. Call it positive mental attitude if you like but I am certain that your mind plays an important part in such proceedings.

Anyway, going back to this particular day, the plaice weren't showing and the skipper soon decided that my shipmates had suffered enough. He knew a spot, round a headland on the way back to port, where conditions would be much more settled and we could, instead, have a go for some bass. At this point, since bass are my favourite fish to catch, I could have rubbed my hands together with glee, especially since, the day before, I had caught some prawns to take with me just in case we stopped at some reefs on the way back to port.

Turning the headland, with about four hours left in the trip, there were some audible sighs of relief at the sight that met our eyes. As if by magic, the swell had been laid to rest and, although there were a few ruffles of wind, in other places the sea might as well have been a mirror. I couldn't wait, especially since I had already replaced the wishbone - my standard plaice rig – at the end of my trace with a fine wire 496BB hook.

And I didn't have long to wait either! Not twenty seconds into the drift and I had a three pounds bass, signalling its murderous intent upon my prawn with a ferocious bang-bang-bang upon the rod tip that was followed by the strike and the wonderful arch of the rod that I so love about this style of fishing. Lunge followed lunge but, a long time ago, I had learned the secret of setting the drag to the point where the fish could take line when it needed while I, in response, never stopped winding.

You see, the secret ally of the bass, in a fight such as this, is slack line. When a bass feels threatened, it flares its gills and shakes its head, trying to do as much damage to its assailant as it can. In a fight with an angler this causes a slight tear in the tissue where the hook has taken hold. Give the fish a bit of slack and the hook will fall straight out.

Constant winding matched to the right setting of the drag avoids this. The only thing that you have got to watch out for is if the bass decides to go on a mad sprint straight towards you. If that happens, you just have to wind like crazy to keep in contact with the fish. Get past that first mad dash however and you will soon have the fish back under control, even on very light tackle.

It works, just as it did on this particular occasion with this particular bass. For him there was going to be no escape, at least not until it had been netted, admired and then released to scrap again another day. I know that they make wonderful eating - and I have no problems with people taking one or two for the pot, even if, nowadays, you have to check the daily bag limits set on recreational anglers – but, for me, I like to put them back alive.

And that set the scene for the rest of the day. Every drift saw me catch a bass, most of them about the same size and just as feisty as the first. I was having a whale of a time and, to be honest, I was so enjoying myself that I was completely oblivious to the effects of my success upon my neighbours. They were still catching the occasional bass, some more than others, most of whom had put on a Storm naturalistic wildeye sandeel, but others weren't having the same degree of …

I was going to write luck just there but, stopping to think about it, it wasn't really. There were plenty of bass to be had, as was evidenced by the fact that we shared a forty seven fish haul between the eight of us. I may have had nineteen of them but this was not because of dazzling skill or blinding good luck but simply because my tackle, my bait and my approach was suited to the fish that we were catching. I had taken the time, the day before, to catch the bait that I was using – live prawns – and I had scaled my tackle down to make it as unobtrusive as possible, which is essential when you are fishing for bass. Any other angler on that boat, doing exactly the same, would have caught just as many fish.

One of the anglers on my right started teasing that I was hogging the best spot on the boat. Now personally I usually enjoy the camaraderie and bit of friendly banter that goes with it. It makes for a nice, enjoyable atmosphere but, with this particular chap, there was an edge of frustration to his voice. It made me curious as to what was going on so I swapped places. It wouldn't make a lot of difference to me, we were in a ten metre boat that was constantly drifting, so shifting six feet to my left wasn't even going to slow me down, but it might make him feel a bit better about his chances.

Now, just as I had suspected, I carried on catching at the same rate that I had before but my companion, despite the move, continued to catch nothing at all. So what was going wrong? I stepped back from the fishing for a little while to see if I could analyse what was happening.

As far as I could see, he was making several mistakes and, for a species like bass, which can be very cautious and often downright faddy, this was almost certainly costing him the chance of a fish.

His line, for example, was thick and coloured. With a strong current in force at the time, he had to put on half a pound of lead to hold the bottom. This meant that, were he to get a bite, he would probably not feel it very well, if at all, while the in your face visibility of both the line and the weight would have put the bass off. By contrast I was using a thin braid with a six metre clear fluorocarbon leader – almost invisible underwater, certainly very hard to spot – and, because of this, I was able to drop down to a three ounce lead weight. Matched to the light baitcaster that I was using, I was able to feel every bump on the bottom while the bass bites themselves were unmistakeable.

Nor did it stop there. For bass, I like to get the hook well away from the rest of the tackle so I use a nine to twelve foot long trace, this time made of 17 pounds breaking strain fluorocarbon. I also use a fine wire hook – a size 2, 496BB – which is so light that it will not interfere with the movements of the bait. In this way the bass see very little coming towards them other than an inviting mouthful that is just asking to be lunch.

By contrast this particular angler was using two short traces on a tackle more suited to whiting. His hooks were large and heavy, his bait was the wrong type for the mark – frozen black lugworms – and even the appeal of these was limited further by the fact that the hooks were so large that they inflicted considerable damage on the worms themselves.

All in all, it lacked finesse, which doesn't matter for species like whiting and dogfish, which can be suicidal, but it did for bass. You need to tempt those into taking! Basically he was fishing with too heavy tackle, too thick line, too cumbersome a rig and the wrong bait. If the plaice had been biting he might have caught one or two – they are far less finicky than bass – but I had my doubts even then. He would have done far better with lighter tackle.

When I am fishing for bass, flatfish or generally smaller species, I scale down to a baitcaster, in this case one with an extremely light six ounce test curve. It is really sensitive to bites, makes the fights sensational and weighs so little that I barely know that I am holding it. It is absolutely brilliant.

It also cost me £14 from a bargain bucket in Trago Mills so who says that good tackle has to be expensive! The reel – a palm sized multiplier – cost a bit more, around £75 if I remember correctly – but even this is very good compared to some of the reels that you can buy. The thing is, as in so many areas, that it pays to shop around.

I use this outfit for all my local drift fishing while I use a saltwater quiver tip – a 1.8m Yuki Cana Surume - for static fishing over reefs and inshore marks with little tide. For anything heavier I use either a six or twelve pounds boat outfit or the lightest uptide boatcaster that I can get away.

As for end tackle, for most of my boat fishing I use a wire boom, which I make myself with stainless steel wire, a pair of mole grips and a pair of pliers. Each boom has a swivel top and bottom and another to the trace. I also put a snap closing weight link on the bottom swivel so that I can change the lead easily, which is something that you have to do when the strength of the tide either increases or decreases.

When the tackle drops into the water, the trace streams away and the arm of the boom rotates to follow it, keeping the trace nice and straight. You do get the occasional tangle but these are few and far between.

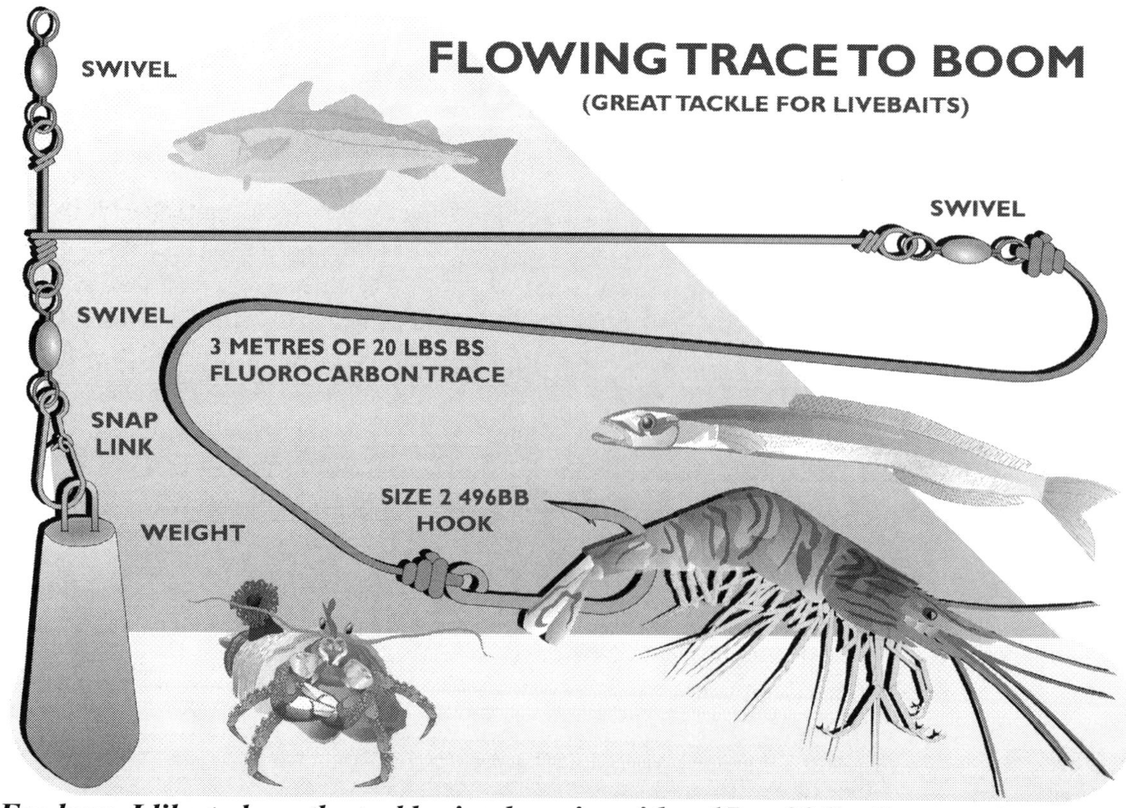

For bass, I like to keep the tackle simple, using either 17 or 20 lbs fluorocarbon trace to make the bait as uncluttered as possible. My homemade booms work well to prevent tangles but there are plenty of commercial ones on the market if you don't fancy making them yourself.

I use the same end tackle for drifting over reefs for pollack and wrasse though I use a different tackle when I am anchored over a reef or rough ground. The rod and reel, however, will need to be matched to the size of the fish that you are likely to encounter.

Light tackle covers a range of outfits. In some places, you can catch big pollack close to the shore – this one was only twenty minutes sail from the harbour – so you need to adopt an outfit capable of dealing with powerful lunges and determined dives for the bottom. As light as possible, certainly, but realistic too. The six ounce baitcaster that I use from my own boat is fine in my home waters, where the pollack are mostly small, but it wouldn't have coped with fish of this size.

For pollack and ballan wrasse, I tend to let the tackle down until it hits the reef then immediately start to retrieve, working my livebait or lure up ten turns from the reef before letting it go down again. They love this approach and will wallop both livebaits and lures hard when you are retrieving. If they don't get hooked, wind slightly faster and **don't** stop. They will think that the prey is getting away and will almost invariably try to hit it again. If you stop winding then you will find that your bait is acting in an unnatural manner and the chances are that the fish will leave it alone.

How far you wind up will also depend on the waters that you are fishing. In deep water, you might encounter wrasse in the first ten to fifteen turns but then continue to encounter pollack up another twenty and, in very deep water, even more than this. It pays to experiment and to remember that every mark is likely to be different.

This pollack hit the lure, missed it and then came back for a second try when I reeled slightly faster. It may feel wrong not to stop and wait but it is the best thing that you can do.

Another advantage of this boom style of rig is that it can be easily adapted for work with other species. When I go plaice fishing, for example, I still use the boom and a nine foot trace but, on the end of it, I tie on a wishbone rig so that I can fish two baits, using them either with bead attractors on both or predator style with beads on the nearer hook and a much larger bait on the hook trailing further away. Both methods work very well but the predator rig tends to sort out the bigger fish.

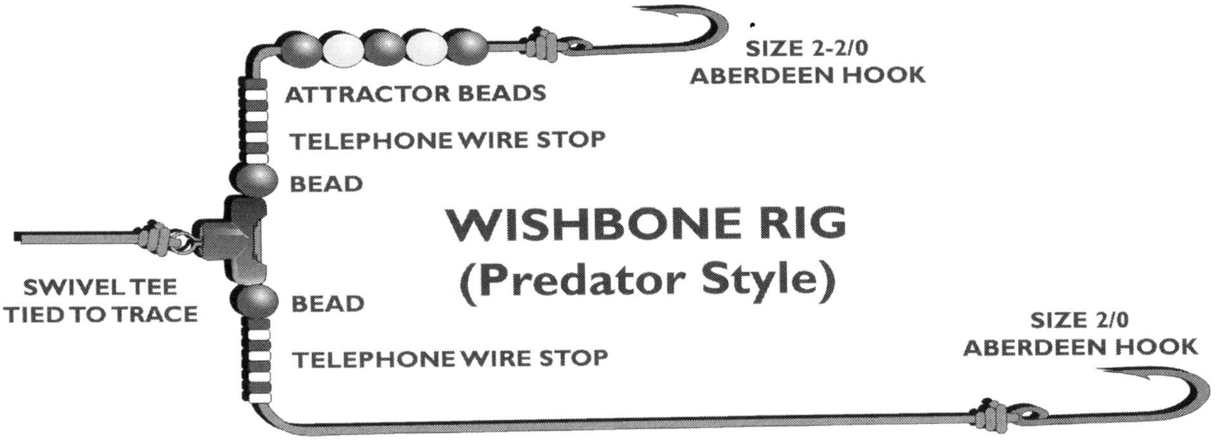

To make the wishbone, you need some telephone wire stops. All you have to do is to get hold of a little bit of telephone wire and strip the outer sheath off the thinner cables inside. Coil the thinner cables around a cake tester or other wire and then cut them into 0.8 centimetre lengths. Slide these onto the line and twist them between your thumb and finger until they grip the line tightly. The tighter you twist, the firmer they grip.

When you make the wishbone, you tie the swivel tee to the long trace and then use another piece of trace to make the wishbone itself, sliding it through the base of the swivel tee and trapping it in place with stops and beads. While I have made the trace stand out by colouring it blue, in practice I use clear fluorocarbon. In regard to distances, I aim for the hook with the beads to be around eight inches (20 cms) from the swivel tee and the plain hook to be around thirty inches (75 cms) away.

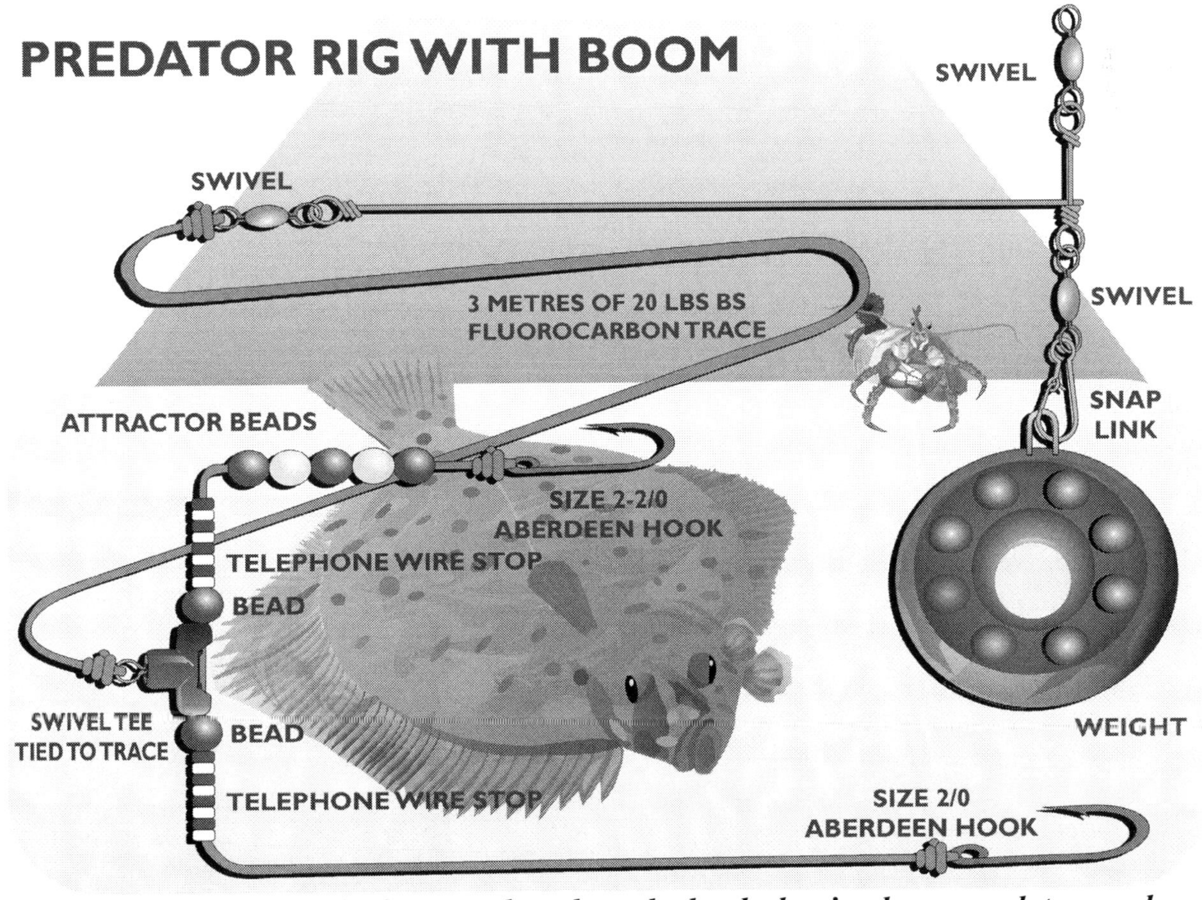

Smaller flatfish tend to be faster so they chase the beads, leaving larger predators such as bigger plaice, turbot and brill to be caught on the trailing second hook.

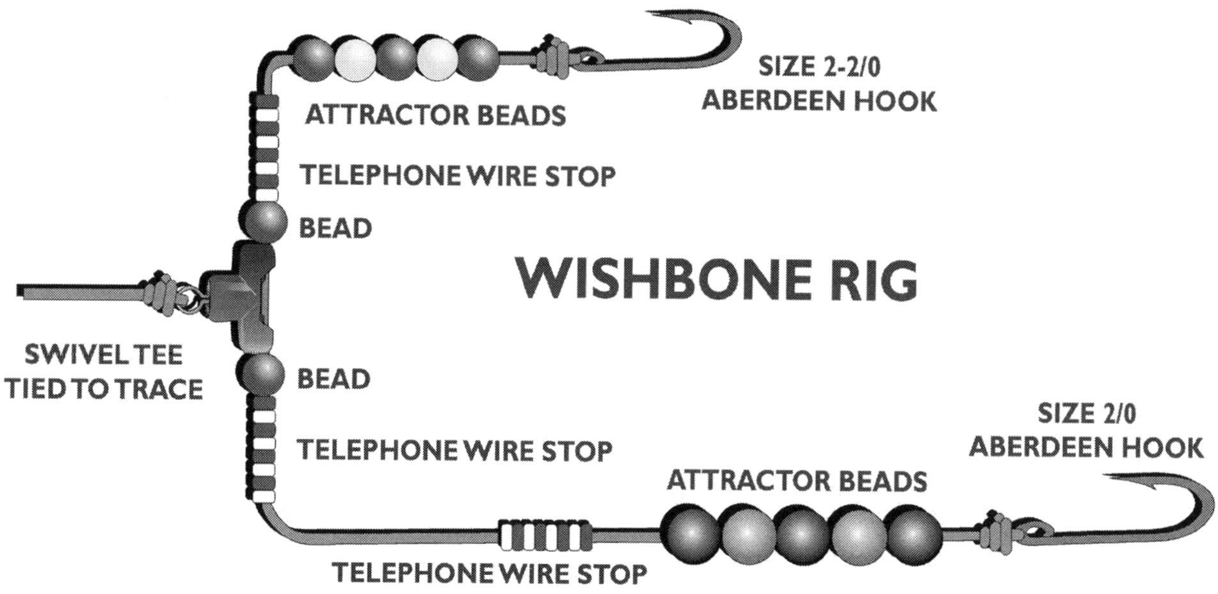

If you use beads on both hooks, match the colour of the beads to the bait. This pattern would be good for ragworms on the near hook and mussels on the other.

For all my plaice fishing, I always put a strip of squid on the hook to act as a visual attractor and add a little bit of scent. The only exception is when I use a predator rig. For this I tend to put a lugworm on the top hook, matched with a strip of squid, but, on the second hook, I put two big lugworms and a long strip of launce (greater sandeel). This is very attractive to bigger flatfish so I tend to make it a generous length, at least six inches (15cms) long and often slightly more.

If you know where there are sandeel netters working in your area, these will often catch launce and will usually freeze them down for pike baits or specimen anglers used to using bigger baits. The strips that they make are really attractive to flatfish – sandeels are, after all, what they are used to feeding on when they are resident on sandbanks – but they are so soft that you will need at least a dozen if you are going to make them last through the day.

You can use squid or cuttlefish instead, cutting the chunky flesh into thin strips that will wave enticingly in the tide, but I only use calamari as a last resort. I far prefer catering squid, with my order of preference being launce, cuttlefish, catering squid and then, and only then, calamari squid as a weapon of last resort.

I have always enjoyed fishing for plaice, letting the tackle all the way down to the bottom and then releasing line so that it follows about fifty or sixty yards behind the boat as it drifts quietly along. Then, when I get a bite, I flip off the spool release and let more line out, counting to ten under my breath before reeling in and feeling the weight of the fish.

At that point, even on lighter tackle, you will usually find that the first stages of the fight that follows is a bit lethargic. The plaice seem quite content to stick to the bottom and follow the tackle in, allowing themselves to be led towards the boat like a dog on a lead. However this soon changes when they find themselves being forced away from the seabed. They don't like this at all and that's when they start to fight in earnest. You will feel their weight properly while the rod will suddenly lunge over as they try to kick their way back down to the bottom. This is the best part of the fight!

When a flatfish does bite, in the majority of cases it will feel almost like a rattle of the rod tip, something with which you will soon become familiar but, occasionally, you will get a much harder, more enthusiastic take that you will need to strike immediately. The culprit for this is usually a gurnard but occasionally it will be another species such as a schoolie (small) bass.

When I have been able to find them, I have found that flat purple beads can be very effective when used with ragworms, as demonstrated by my young friend above. I have shown my favourite combination below.

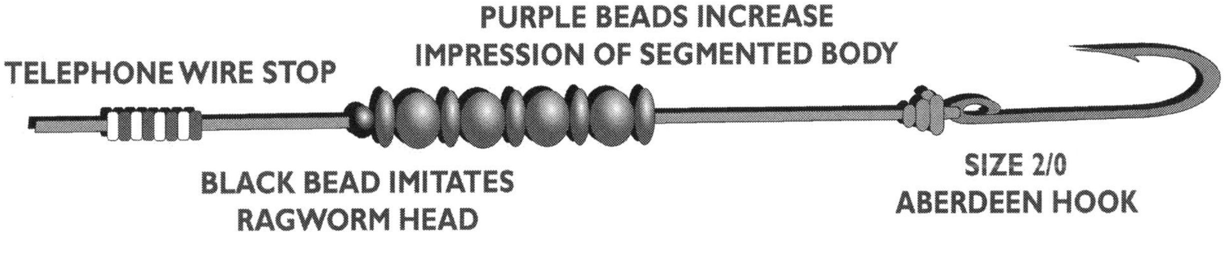

Whenever I have imagined flatfish attacking a ragworm, I have always thought it logical that they will strike at the opposite end to the pincers. I may well be wrong but the addition of the little black bead has certainly not had a detrimental effect upon my catches!

If you are drifting over sandy ground for flatfish, you will often find that red and tub gurnard will take the bait, especially if you are using squid strip with peeler crab. You can tell them apart by the blue border on the pectoral fins of the tub.

Fishing over sand and mud will also bring you into range of other species such as smooth-hounds. These tend to be fished for at anchor and, once again, I will bring one of my booms into play, albeit with a much stronger hook baited with half a crab and a strip of squid as a visual and scent attractor. For these I sometimes experiment with lure rods, especially if their average size is fairly small, but, if the big boys are around, then I will reach for either my uptide or my 12 pounds class outfits, both of them matched to multipliers loaded with braid and thirty pounds breaking strain fluorocarbon tippet. These have got a bit more backbone to them and will enable me to put some extra pressure on the fish when I am playing them in.

Whenever I have caught a smooth-hound, they have hit the bait hard so I have struck both immediately and just as hard to set the hook firmly. They give a very hard fight and can be great fun to play in. Unfortunately, in some areas, they tend to congregate where there is a lot of tide, which means using heavier weights than I normally like. This is why I have got the uptide and twelve pound class outfits. They are much stronger than the tackle that I normally prefer but they are lighter by far than many of the outfits that I have seen people use.

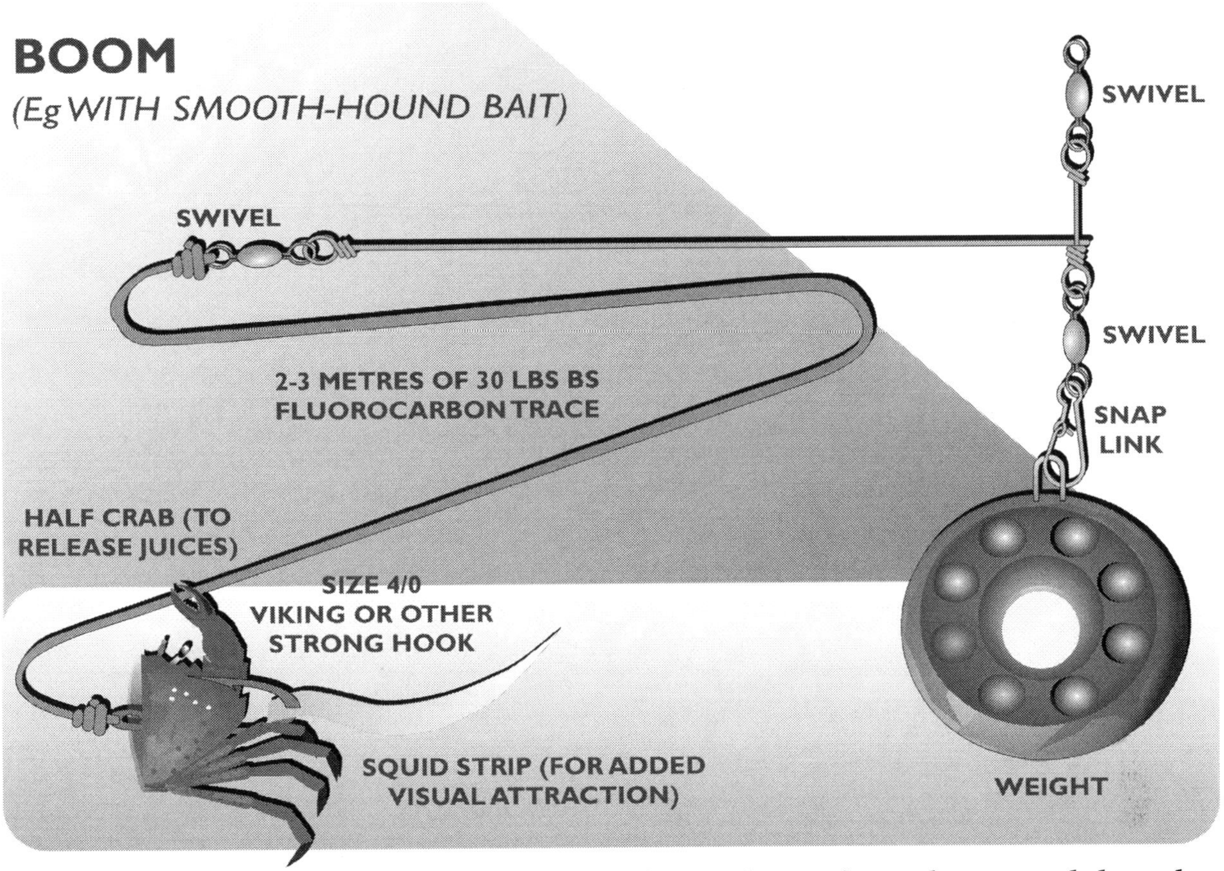

Booms are also good for when you are anchoring up for species such as smooth-hounds. Notice the weight though. I use watch leads over sand for plaice and smooth-hounds but pears or arlesey bombs when I am fishing for bass.

In a lot of places around the UK – and indeed in many other parts of the world – people like to anchor up over areas either on or close to reefs, especially when there are bream around. These hard-fighting fish tend to be very quick biting and, with their relatively small mouths, can be quite hard to hook. I love fishing for them and find that a rod fitted with a saltwater quiver tip is just about perfect both for hooking them and for getting a good fight out of them afterwards.

The tackle, however, is very different. There are so many snags and clumps of weed around that long traces are just asking for trouble. Nor do the bream seem to mind shorter traces, especially if you float them off the bottom with a large buoyant bead above the rig. This helps to float the hooks into easy sight of the bream and also helps to keep the tackle away from potential snags.

The tackle that I use, since I am targeting smaller species, is a three hook paternoster made with four way clear beads. These not only help to minimise visual clutter around the baits but also help to keep everything sorted out and untangled. I have found, even when the tide is racing, that the tackle works well with the added advantage that it is a cheap rig to make and even easier to use. It certainly works well for bream but also has the advantage of taking many other species as well. In the winter, for example, it can wreak havoc on the whiting!

The stops in use on both the rig body and the traces are tied out of the actual nylon. They are also very simple. Just make a loop, turn the end back on itself and go around the doubled strands four or five times. Pull tight and the resulting knot should be too large to pull through the beads. (If you are using a fine diameter line, double check this before you put the tackle in the water. You may need to up it depending on what you find.) You will need to tie one of these knots both above and below the four way bead to trap it in place. This applies to both your traces and the rig body itself which, for durability, I tie out of 30 lbs bs fluorocarbon.

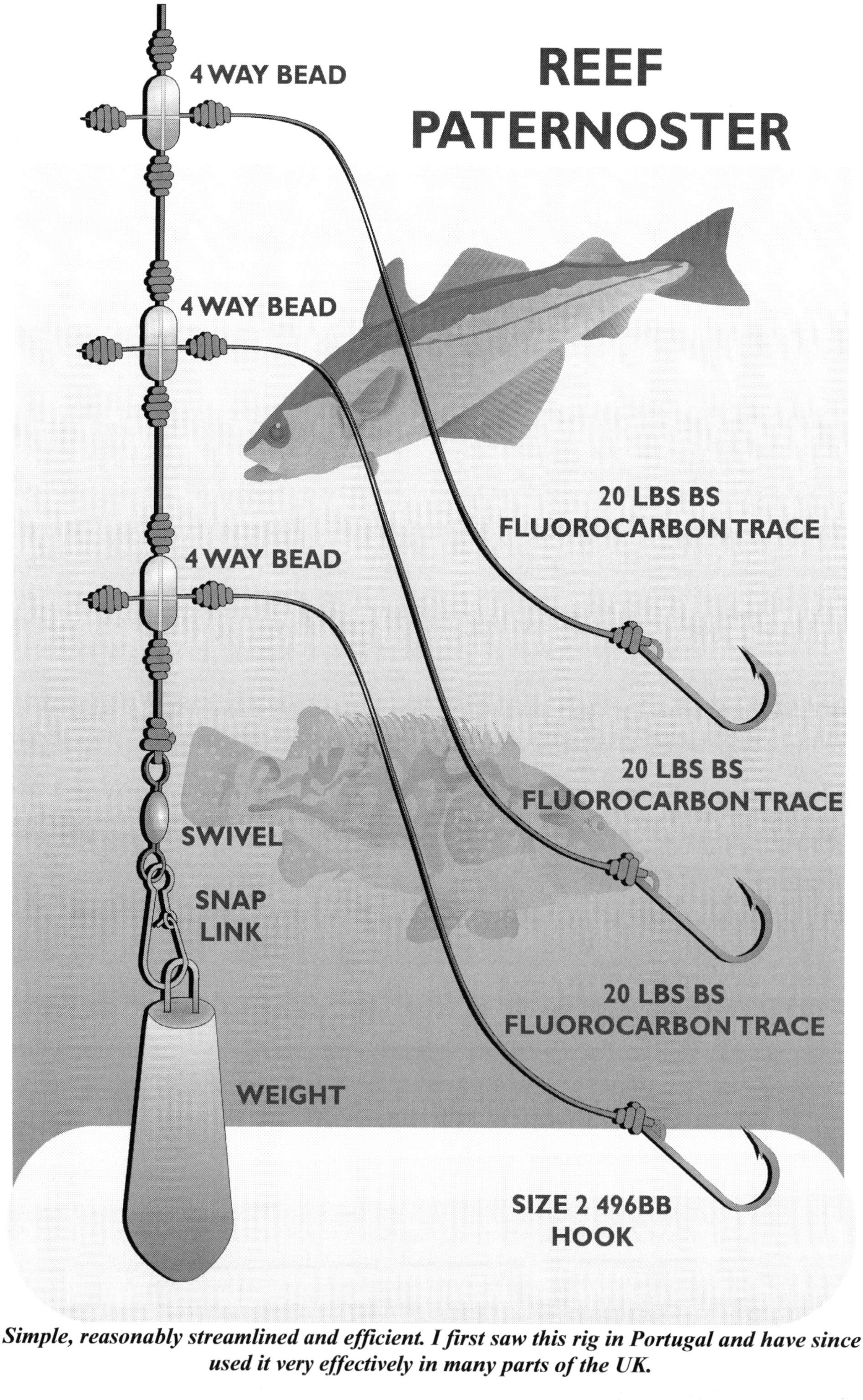

Simple, reasonably streamlined and efficient. I first saw this rig in Portugal and have since used it very effectively in many parts of the UK.

The method of fishing this style of tackle is also just about as simple as it is possible to get. Let it down to the bottom, feel for bites and hit them when they happen. Reel up, rebait and get your tackle down again to have another go.

As far as bait is concerned, there are a variety of things that you can try, from ragworms, lugworms, chunks of tiger prawns and strips of squid with different baits working well for different species. Most of the time I tend to use ragworms tipped with strips of squid but another angler that I know swears by mussels. In Portugal they use chunks of prawn and, judging from the reports of people who have been successful using this bait from the shore, I see no reason why it should not be successful over here.

The boat that I went on in Portugal - the Jose Batista - was arranged by Wish & Fish and was palatial by comparison to some of the English charter boats that I have been on. It was also where I first saw this style of paternoster used to devastating effect!

My favourite, when I have time to collect them after a storm, is chunks of razorfish. Bream seem to love them but wrasse are also happy to cheerfully munch upon them too. Basically you open the shell, bring out the foot, chop it into smaller pieces and then secure it to the hook using baiting elastic.

When you get a fish, it will put a very satisfying bend on the rod as you bring it up to the boat, fighting all the way and putting up a very spirited performance. Also, since these fish travel in shoals, you can find yourself catching quite a few in a short period of time. Of course you also get the opposite, when the shoal has travelled away from where you are fishing, but that's just the way it goes. You could try to move the boat about and chase them but, on the whole, that's not really productive.

Since bream tend to be fairly territorial, their patrols will bring them back around to where you are fishing often enough to keep up both your interest and your enthusiasm. Sometimes you can even trigger bites just by flicking your tackle a little further out. When I was in

Portugal, I found that all of the bites came from a ten foot section of reef. Even a yard or two out either side saw the bites completely dry up and vanish. You had to be exactly on the mark.

Since then, probably because I have been watching for this particular behaviour, I have often found myself having similar experiences over here. However, during the lulls in activity, there are usually other species around so it is a good idea to change your bait and see what change of fortune this brings. It is never over, as they say, until the fat lady sings, the fat lady in this case being the throaty roar of the engine as you head back to port!

Saul, the crewman on the Jose Batista, after scarpa, a type of bream. Just look at the bend of the rod and that should be enough to tell you why I love lighter tackle.

Pole fishing can be a great way to introduce children to angling. My grandchildren used to love it when they were younger.

One of the best ways that I know to introduce children to angling is to get them catching fish, preferably easily, quickly and, whenever possible, lots of them! Pole fishing, with both its simplicity and the added visual element of a float, tends to fit this bill admirably, even though it is a tactic virtually unknown in the sea today. It's a shame really. Just look at old, pre-war photographs around many areas and you will see that it is a method that hundreds, if not thousands of people used to use. What do you think they did before rods were invented? Not any more though. Today it is a tactic that most people don't even bother to think about.

And it is such a shame. It's cheap, it's fun and it can be really hectic. We had one day, for example, when we – myself and two grandchildren – had 127 fish in just over an hour and a half. That's not bad going, especially since that ten species haul included golden grey mullet and wrasse to two and a half pounds!

You have got to be quick with the wrasse. Get them up and away from the snags or they will break you off in a matter of seconds!

Personally, I thoroughly enjoy pole fishing, even though it does get you a few odd looks and the occasional person looking down their nose at you. Not that that tends to last very long. Quite often, when we have been catching well, we find ourselves having to contend with conventional anglers dropping their floats all around us in the hopes of catching some of the fish that we have been steadily releasing. They can be a pest but I do understand. Why should we have all the fun?

So, how do you start, what do you do and how much does it cost? The first step has got to be finding a pole. I started my grandchildren off with four metre whips that I bought for seven pounds each. Then, when they were a bit older, we moved up to five metres - £12 - with six and seven metre poles in reserve for when we were targeting bass and wrasse. And yes, that's not a typo, we have had quite a few bass over the years, especially when we have been using prawns. They come a lot closer to the shore than many people might think and we have had them, on the pole, to just over four and a half pounds.

We have also had plaice, flounders, golden grey mullet, mackerel, scad, herring, garfish, bream, both red and black, ballan wrasse and pollack, not to mention a wide range of mini species. Makes you think, doesn't it?

You can get hold of some really cheap poles but, generally, the stiffer ones with slightly stronger tips come in at around the £20 mark. Bit more perhaps for a seven metre but, as in all things, you get what you pay for. For myself, I tend to go cheap and cheerful, especially since they can break on you occasionally. It all depends how you treat them. I think, between the eight of us that regularly use them, we have broken about six in twenty years, which isn't that bad.

After you have bought your pole, you have got to get it ready for sea fishing. To do that, you need to pull out the eye that comes with the pole and throw it away. They rust in next to no time and are completely inadequate for the fight that you can get from a species like wrasse. Instead take a six inch length of stainless steel wire, fold it in half to make an eye, crimping the last five or six millimetres slightly downwards, and then whip it in position with whipping thread. Seal it with superglue or cellulose dope, let it dry and then cover it with araldite rapid or other quick drying resin, remembering to rotate the blank as it dries so that the resin forms a nice smooth coat rather than a botch job with unsightly sagging and wrinkling.

Don't be too quick putting it on the cellulose or superglue either. Put it on before the base coat cures properly and the resin turns milky white, which completely spoils its appearance.

If you haven't done a whipping before, have a look at the diagram below, which I'll follow with step by step instructions.

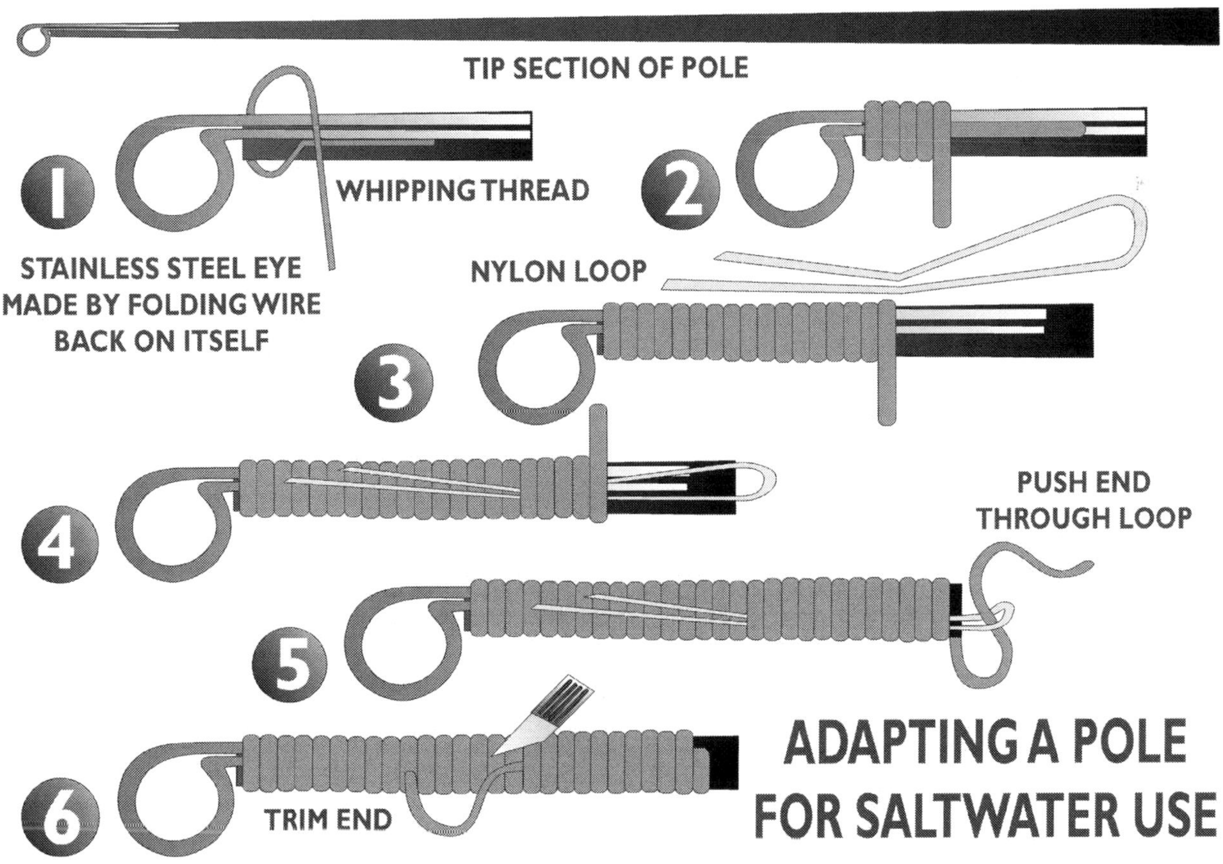

1. Lay the wire next to the pole tip. You are going to secure it in position by wrapping whipping thread around it so you need to trap the end of the thread with the first few turns. After three or four you can normally pull the coils nice and tight.

2. Keep going, wrapping round and round the pole until you are about a centimetre away from the end of the wire.

3. Double a six inch length of nylon back on itself to make a loop. Lay it next to the pole.
4. Trap the loop beneath the rest of the turns that you are going to make. You want it covered by the whipping thread.

5. When you have reached the end of the wire, make a few turns beyond and then tuck the end through what's left of the protruding loop.

6. Pull the loop through and out of the whipping, dragging the end of the thread with it. Pull everything tight and trim with a sharp knife. Seal it in the way that I have already described.

If you want a really smooth transition from the wire legs to the blank you can always, when you make the new eye, use a file to make a little slope at the end of the wire but that's up to you. Thicker thread, rather than ultra thin nylon, makes the job a bit easier too.

Your next job is to buy some pole elastic – I use red hollow elastic rated 13-16 or bigger – and make some links for your end tackle. Since we are not using internal elastic, which stretches too far for some of the grudge matches that you are going to have with wrasse, these links are going to act as extra shock absorbers between you and the fish.

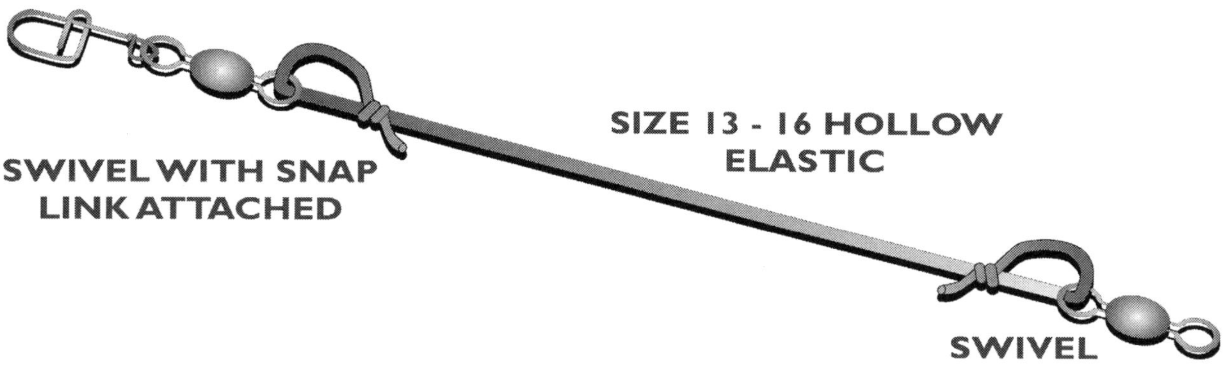

To make them you thread the elastic through the eye of the swivel and then, holding the swivel and using it to stretch the elastic, secure the swivel in place with a loop knot (not the blood bight loop mentioned in Chapter 3). Repeat at both ends.

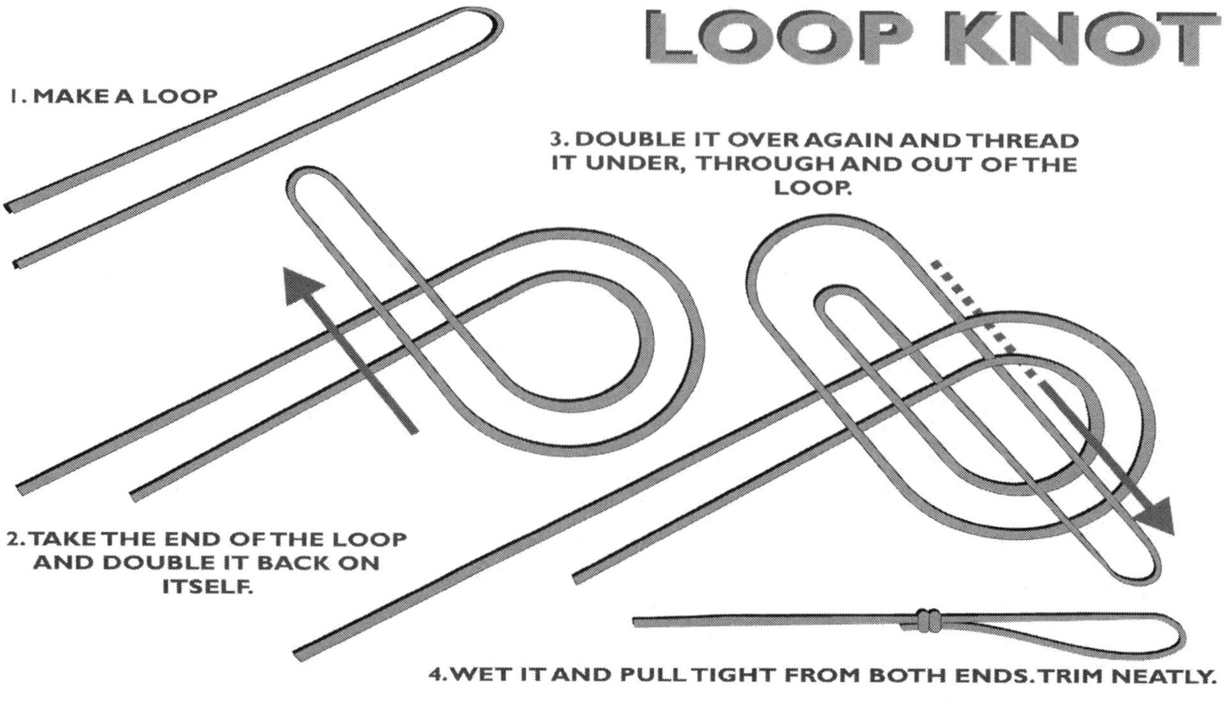

You are now ready to tie on your actual tackle, for which you are going to make a rig body using fifteen to seventeen pounds breaking strain fluorocarbon. Tie this to the swivel at one end of your elastic link and use the snap link to connect the elastic to the eye of the pole. Place the fluorocarbon against the pole and measure out a length that is about four feet shorter than the pole itself. Your basic float tackle will then be a conventional float rig – albeit scaled down - and you can, if you like, use a telephone wire stop instead of a stop knot.

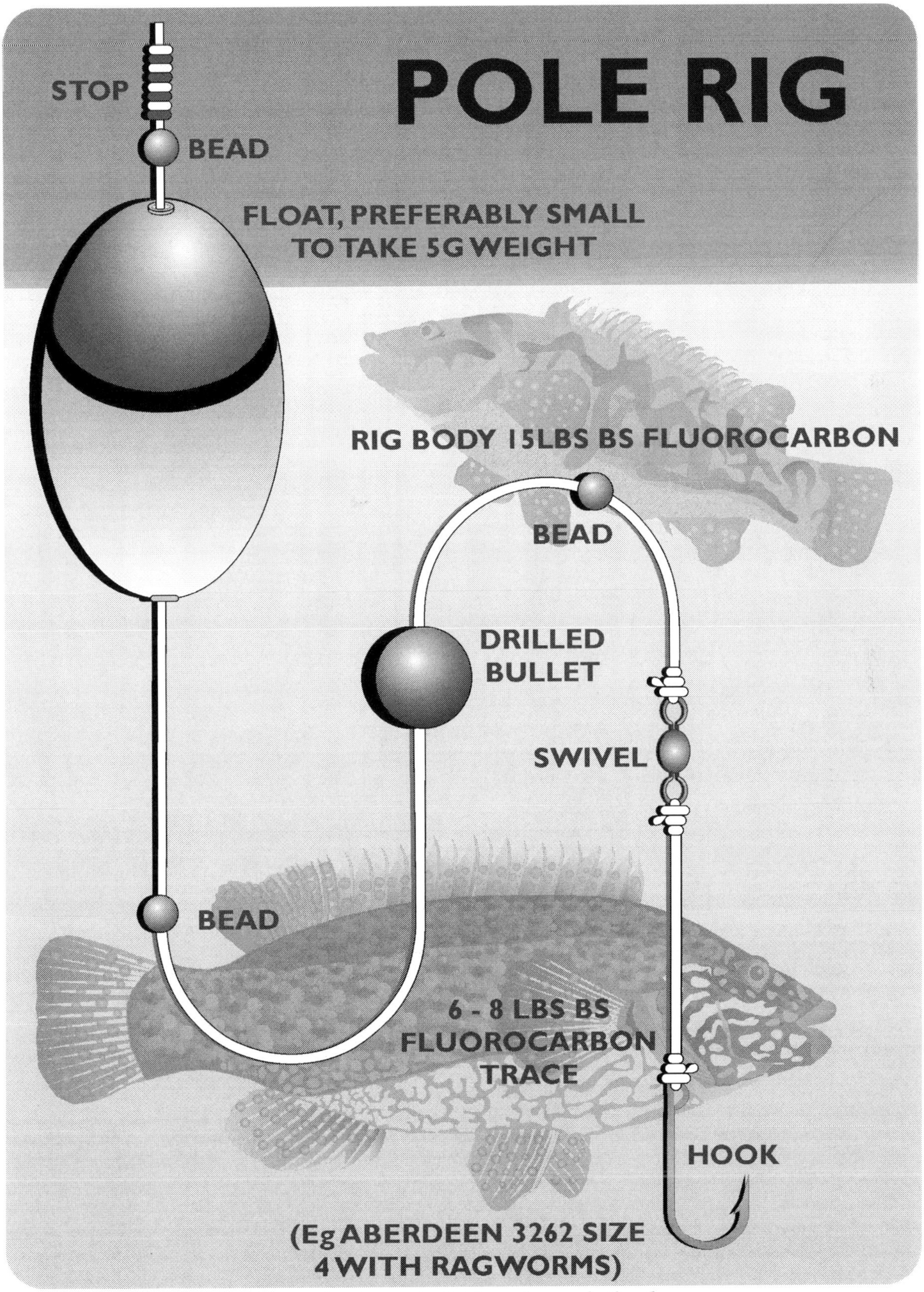

Float rig for pole fishing through the day.

I haven't gone into specific sizes for the floats because, to a certain extent, that is going to be dictated by what you can find. Personally I go for floats that will balance with five to seven gram weights. These are much smaller than the floats that I use for mackerel fishing and so, because of their light resistance, any bites that you get will be considerably magnified. The float just disappears underwater, giving you plenty of time to strike. I think that is one of the reasons why children love this style of fishing; it is just so visually exciting.

When you are ready to tie on your trace, this should be the right length so that your hook touches the butt cap at the end of the pole. What hook you put on will then depend on what you want to catch. If I am going for garfish, mackerel, scad or pollack, I will use a Kamasan B980 size 2 hook. If I am going for wrasse, I will use an Aberdeen 3262 size 4 hook with ragworms while, if I am using prawns for bass and larger wrasse and pollack, I will use a size 2 496BB hook which is light enough not to interfere with the movements of the prawn.

Prawns will often tempt bigger wrasse, which will put a terrific bend in a four metre pole.

But it will cope with most of them, just as it did with this two and a quarter pounder.

When you are ready to start fishing, just hold the pole up, lift it slightly towards you, enough to get the tackle moving, and then give it a swing away from you, following it down as the tackle lands in the water. Whether or not you get bites will then not only depend on how many fish there are around but how deep you have set your float. If I am fishing for wrasse, for example, I will then experiment with the depth until the hook is about a foot off the bottom. This is also where I target bass with live prawns.

I remember on one occasion, quite a while ago now, when my daughter and my eldest grandson came with me for a quick trip to a mark in Paignton. He was very keen and quite surprised when bites weren't instant. However, as I told him then, just keep making sure that you put the float back into exactly the same place every time.

'I'm not getting any bites there,' he said, slightly puzzled. 'What's the point of that?'

The thing is, as I explained to him, wrasse are a territorial species but they also seem to have a pretty good sense of smell. You may start off with few bites but, as the scent starts to disperse in the water, so the fish will follow the trail until they come to where the scent is strongest, ie where your bait is. It may take a little while but, eventually, their numbers will grow and, as they become more emboldened, so too will the numbers of bites.

A few seconds later, as if on cue, his float dipped beneath the surface. A quick bob, you might say, which was followed by the first of a few mini-species including blennies, shannies and gobies. Not really my cup of tea but an inevitable bycatch of this particular method. Then, as the tide grew higher, with us changing our depth to stay in that foot off the bottom region, the bites started getting more aggressive with corkwing and rainbow wrasse making an appearance.

My grandson, now that the fish were getting bigger, was quite happy, though he was taken by surprise when the first ballan appeared. At just over a pound and a quarter, it put a decided bend in the pole before we were able to get it into the landing net, an accessory which is a must for all light tackle fishing. You are, after all, using fairly delicate rods and poles, not cranes, and you need to bear this in mind if you are going to get the best from them.

This is especially true of poles. If you get hooked up on the bottom, you need to point the pole straight towards the obstruction and pull. Don't point it up and expect the pole to be strong enough to pull you free or break the trace. It won't be and it is a surefire recipe for a broken pole. One of the reasons that I use telescopic, rather than put together poles, is that I can collapse them quickly, get hold of the swivel at the bottom of the link and use this to pull free from snags. If it comes free, you can push the pole out and be fishing again within seconds or, if the trace has broken, well that won't take long to fix either.

Both are preferable to a broken pole.

You also need to be aware of what's going on behind you. If the tackle comes free suddenly it can shoot backwards with frightening speed. I always turn my head away and double check that there is no-one walking behind me when I pull. I also make sure that I am wearing my glasses, which are fitted with shatter proof lenses to protect my eyes, and I try to remember a baseball cap to help protect my head.

Anyway, on this particular day we caught quite a few fish – I know that Tiernan had well over forty because he didn't let me forget it for quite a while – bless! - but between the three of us we must have had over a hundred. I had caught thirty seven and I don't think Becky bothered to count, despite swinging them in one after the other. It was a good day.

But it was a short trip. Light was fading fast and I remember wishing that I had thought of a way to carry on fishing in the dark. Wrasse, being a diurnal species, wouldn't be on the target list but this mark was well known for scad and there was always the chance of some good pollack, not to mention herring and pout, which were sometimes big enough to be interesting, at least at this particular spot. Hum… Something to think about.

Which is why, when I got home, I went straight onto the internet to see what was around. There had to be something better than the clumpy accessories that I had previously designed for mackerel fishing. I just felt that they would be too clumsy for fishing on the pole. I wanted a more elegant solution.

As it turned out, there were a variety of night floats around, some of them self-weighted, which would be okay for float-fished live sandeels for bass but not for much else, and a lot of them very expensive. Then I found a pack of three for 99p, which must have appealed to the miserly side of my nature because I ordered them straight away.

The thing is, at 33p each I wouldn't have been a lot out of pocket if they had been absolutely rubbish. The idea behind them sounded feasible enough. When the float was dipped into water, a circuit was made with two fine wire filaments and the light came on. Take it out of the water and the light went off but put it back in again and the float would stay illuminated for a period of up to twelve hours.

To rig the floats, I was going to need a bit of silicon tubing so that they could be fastened in the same way that you do a lot of coarse floats. If they worked, they would also need a few split shot to make sure that they sank to the right level. However, considering how slim they were, they might be even more effective than the dumpy little floats that I was using through the day. They would be no good for livebaits but could be very good for mackerel strip.

And, much to my delight, they worked perfectly, meaning that we could extend the use of the poles into the dark. Since then I have continued to use them, not only for general night fishing but also to collect bait although, to be truthful, that was initially a bit of a surprise. I found that out, early one morning, when I put a tiny strip of mackerel on an equally tiny hook just to see if there were any herring around. There weren't but I ended up with twenty or so sand smelts. I was well chuffed with that, especially since these lively little fish, as shiny as they are energetic, are some of the best bass baits that you are ever likely to encounter.

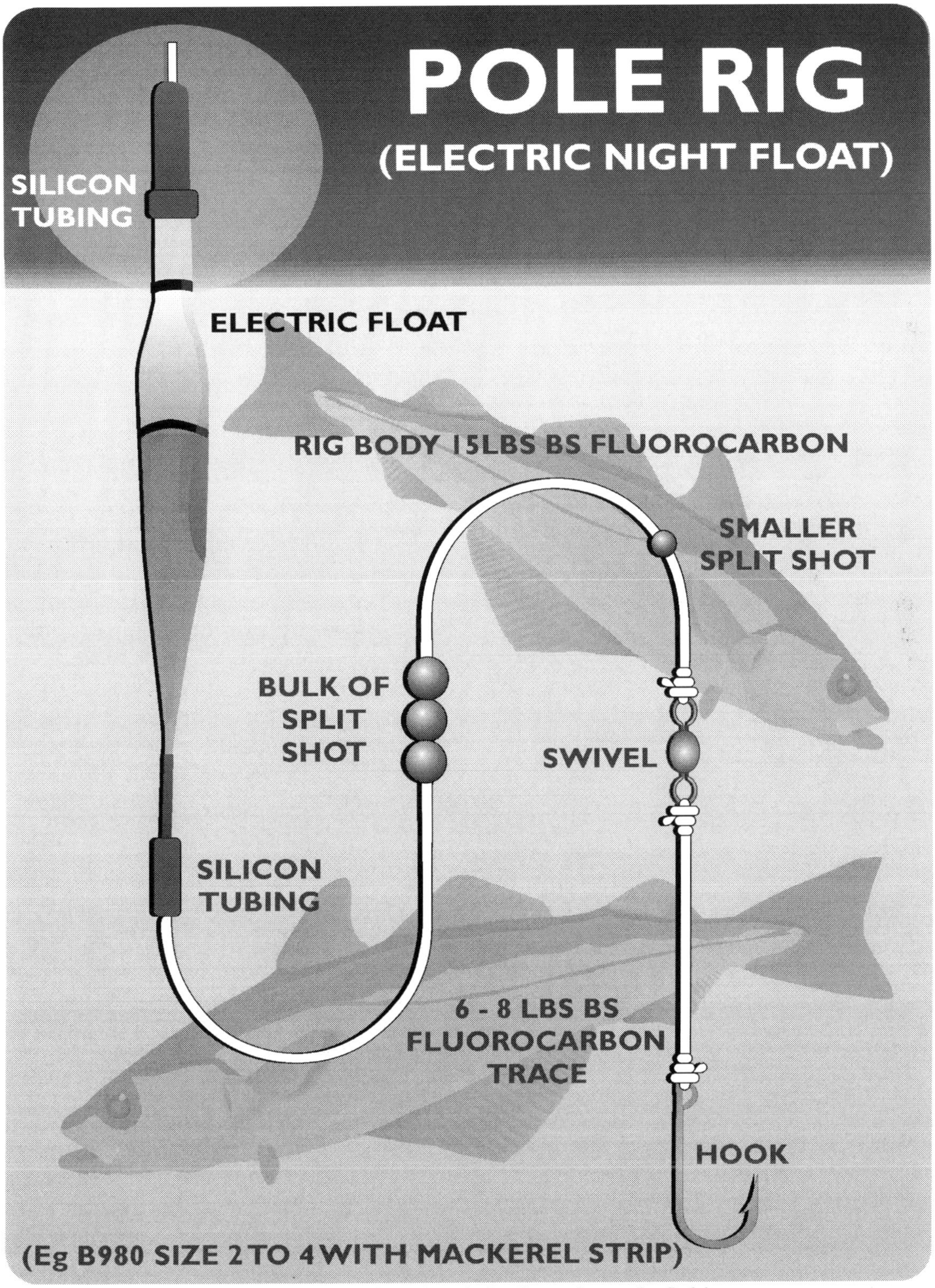

How to rig an electric night float for pole fishing.

So score one more for the poles! Not that I needed any convincing. One thing that I have seen over and over again in my angling career is that fish often come much closer to the shore than many people might think. Okay, in the majority of cases you want a good depth of water, making headlands, piers and harbour walls ideal places from which to use the poles, but even then there are exceptions.

I remember, one Summer, when I had so many flounders close in that I decided to see if I could catch them on the pole, pushing a couple of bank sticks into the sand at the side of the estuary and fitting out a seven metre pole with a tiny leger outfit rather than a float. To hedge my bets, I popped out a conventional rig on a bass rod as well but you may imagine my surprise when I caught five flounders and a specimen silver eel on the pole and a solitary flounder on the rod!

The thing is, they can be good fun and, as a weapon in your light tackle armoury, they well deserve a place. Add in their appeal to children, the fact that they are so inexpensive and that they often catch fish when other methods don’t and hopefully you will begin to understand their appeal. You see, in fishing, there is no one size fits all solution but, to my way of thinking, a variety of interesting methods servicing a wide range of potential experiences is likely to be a lot more fun anyway. Why don’t you give it a go and see what you think?

Chapter Eight: Pier Fishing Transformation

While it would be lovely to be able to go fishing and hook big fish all year round, in real life it doesn't work like that. Time of the year and the ever turning seasons mean that there are months when the fishing, while it can still be enjoyable, tends only to produce a similarly-sized run of small to medium fish.

In Torbay, the quietest month tends to be March, just after the winter fish have moved into deeper water and just before the summer species start turning up in any real numbers. Many of my friends call it the doldrums month and some don't bother to fish it at all.

Personally I think that this is a real shame, especially when, if you're prepared to lower your sights a bit, you can still have a great deal of fun. The other night was a prime example. I had a couple of hours free so I decided to go fishing down at Babbacombe Pier. This tends to hold a reasonable stock of dogfish and there is always the chance of other species turning up like whiting, bull buss, three bearded rockling and congers. I have also had dabs and thornback rays down there too.

The drive down there and back is a bit interesting, with the road in a shocking state and, in one place in particular, potentially dangerous. However, once you're down, it's a very short walk to the end of this miniature pier, which makes it ideal for trips when your time is very limited.

Bearing in mind that the weather was grim and that we had just entered the doldrums month of March, I wanted to get the most out of every fish that I was going to catch. Consequently I took with me my Portuguese beachcaster, a 4.5m Eurocaster rated for casting weights up to 100g that I had bought a couple of years previously while on holiday in Albufiera, and a Shimano Nexave beachcaster, also 4.5m and similarly rated at 100g casting weight.

These rods are terrific fun when the tide is light enough to enable you to hold bottom with a three ounce spiked lead. They are not designed for four ounces, though I have seen the Nexave, which is available in Britain, advertised with a casting range of 2 – 4 ozs. That is a response – in my opinion a very ill-advised response - by tackle retailers to the typical British attitude of wanting tackle capable of manhandling in every fish that is caught. The attitude seems to be that '100g is close enough to four ounces so that British anglers will think that they will be fine for most beachcasting marks and then we will sell more of them.'

And it's rubbish. On one of the angling forums a chap was bemoaning the fact that his Nexave, along with what seemed a long list of other rods, had broken on him – and I'm not surprised! Even an ordinary lob with a four ounce weight, in the hands of someone who knows what he, or she, is doing, is asking for trouble. These rods are **not** designed for casting four ounce leads. They are basically saltwater quiver tips – rods designed with light, sensitive tips that are capable of significantly enhanced bite detection under the right circumstances, ie where there is a light tide and a three ounce weight will hold bottom. Used correctly, they can provide hours of dazzling entertainment but they are not designed to be thrashed with a weight rated at more than they are capable of casting - and thank goodness for it! That would turn them into the same sort of thick, soulless beachcasters that the majority of sea anglers use – not, I think, because that is what they particularly want but simply because that is what is generally available and no-one has ever told them anything different.

Used correctly, as I was doing on this particular night, and they can give you wonderful sport, transforming your fishing. You need to take a little more care but, as every sportsman in every other discipline than angling will tell you, when you have got decent equipment, you need to look after it. (Unlike the rough and ready fishing approach of thrash it and trash it.)

Care with light beachcasters is essential. When I am fishing at Babbacombe, or anywhere where there is a wall to lean on, I use a padded pole rest rather than a tripod or the wall itself. You can pick them up very cheaply too. This one was around £17.

Anyway, going back to my selection of tackle, I match both of my rods with light, decent quality baitrunners loaded with fifteen pounds breaking strain monofilament and a 50lbs bs clear monofilament leader. Since I follow the Angling Trust guidelines of no more than three hooks between two rods, I rigged the Eurocaster up with a straightforward running leger and the Nexave with a two hook paternoster made up in the same way as my reef rig but with slightly stronger, and therefore stiffer, fluorocarbon.

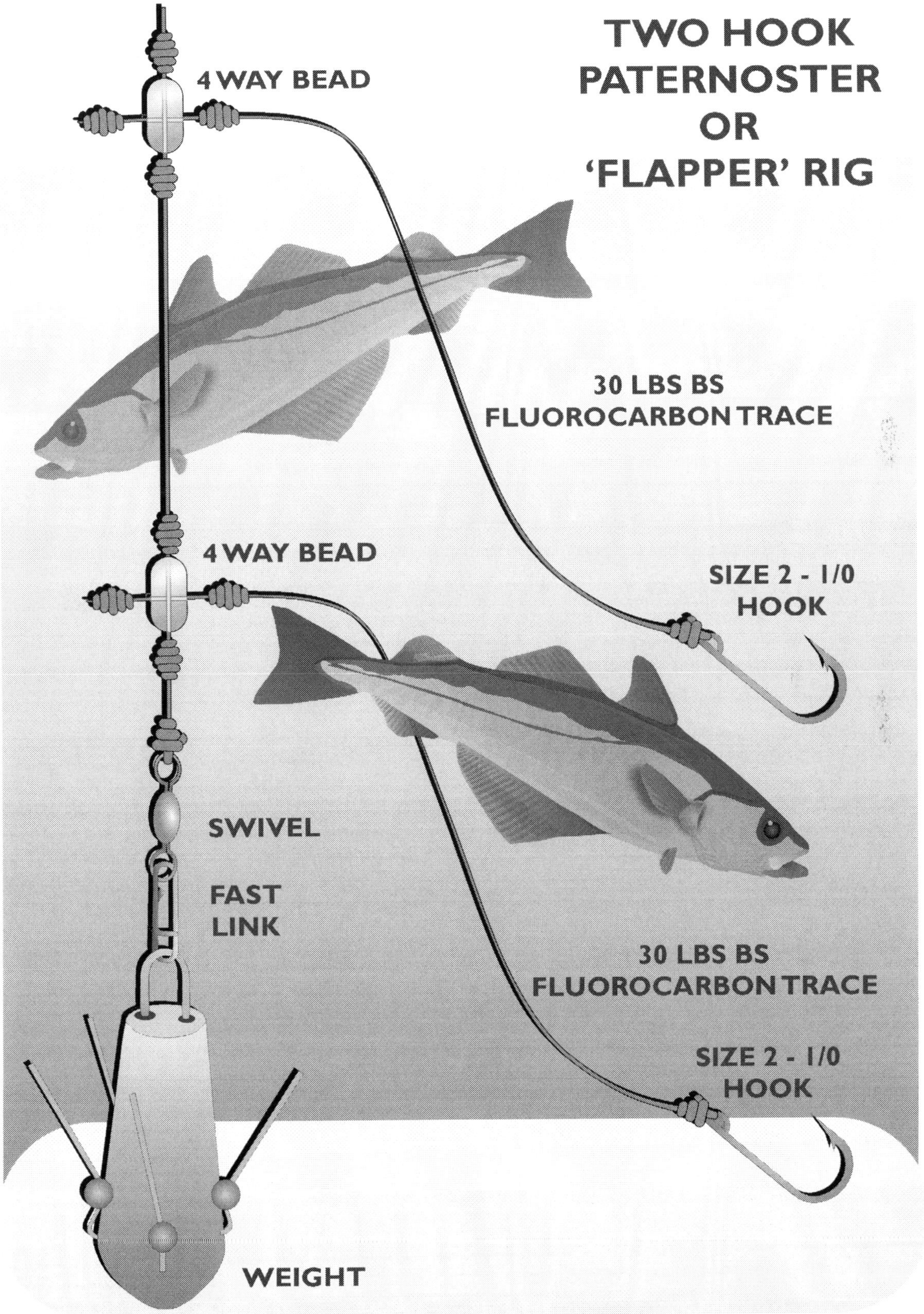

Using stiffer fluorocarbon for the traces will stop the majority of tangles when you are casting. After all, the dynamics of hurling a rig out to sea or simply dropping it quietly over the side of the boat are very, very different.

I sliced the mackerel that formed part of my bait into medium slices and used these to bait the paternoster. A little tip here though, if you ever want to buy mackerel for bait, either buy frozen or tell the fishmonger that you want it for sushi and need the freshest possible fish. Whatever you are doing, don't tell them that you want it for bait. More than once, when I was younger, I made this mistake, whereupon the fishmonger disappeared into a back room and reappeared moments later with a newspaper wrapped bag that would, when I opened it later, contain a disgusting mush of mackerel that was not fit for eating and certainly not fit for bait.

To add to the cheek of it, they would inevitably have charged full price for what was nothing other than decomposing trade waste. Needless to say, I never went back to those shops again while the memory has stuck with me ever since.

On my other rod I put a whole, albeit fairly small, squid and, while on this subject, another note of caution. Some shops – and I would like to think that they are in a very small minority - buy squid in bulk, defrost it and then make up a number of small packets for sale as crab bait. The remaining squid are then put back into larger bags and refrozen. However, by this time the flesh has usually turned pink instead of white and it has also softened considerably from the tougher firmness that you would normally expect from fresher squid.

So, when you buy squid, check that the flesh is white. If it isn't, don't buy it. The squid will be soft and fly off your hook far too easily. You could, of course, fix it in position by securing it with baiting elastic, but, to be honest, I'd sooner have tougher, fresher bait.

Casting out, I soon got the familiar quick rattle of a small whiting but, on the Nexave, even this could be felt trying hard to reach the bottom which, on a conventional beachcaster, you just wouldn't experience. Such whiting are often too small to make an impression on the heavier blanks of such a rod. Another point of interest however is that their initial bites, on the lighter tips of these continental rods, are much more magnified. This means that they are spotted quickly, struck and hooked before they get a chance to gorge the bait. That has the advantage of far more surviving than many other anglers would expect.

Hooked cleanly in the mouth, this whiting has a much better chance of survival.

As dusk turned into darkness, I was joined by another angler, just as the dogfish came on the feed. First up was one of the smallest bull huss that I have ever seen, which was quickly returned to live and fight another day.

You can tell that this camera shy dogfish is a male by the claspers. (Bottom right) Dogfish often curl up like this when captured or, in the wild, when they are threatened by danger.

Sometimes, telling a small bull huss apart from a lesser spotted dogfish can be a little tricky since they tend to have similar bodies and the spots – larger and more widely spaced on a huss – aren't as pronounced on the smaller fish. What you need to do is to hold the tail firmly by the fish's head, so that you do not get an abrasion from their sandpaper skin and their muscular squirming, and turn them over. Take a close look at their mouths and their nasal flaps, or lobes, which are immediately above the mouth. On a bull huss the nasal flaps form two distinct lobes which do not reach the mouth. On a lesser spotted dogfish their lobes form into one, the corners of which do reach the mouth.

Looking at the picture above, it reminds me of quite frequent occasions when I have heard people say remarks along the lines of 'you can understand why they call them dogfish.' Yes, they do curl up in the same way, but this is not where their name comes from. Actually people used to believe that they hunted in packs, like many species of wild and domesticated dogs, and that's why they called them dogfish!

Which were now coming in regularly while my companion alternated between living on the phone – what is it with young people and their phones? – and reeling them in at high speed. When I next caught a dogfish – a lesser this time – he stopped to watch, telling whoever was on the other end of his phone that 'the bloke down here had caught a big one' since 'his rod was bent right over.' Later on this was changed to the less gratifying 'he's got a floppy rod!'

But I was having fun! On these rods, even a two pound dogfish puts up a significant fight. You have got to lift the rod steadily, exerting extra pressure by using the left hand on the front of the blank both to steady and lighten the strain on the right hand, then wind smoothly down in time with the lowering of the rod. This will enable you to fight larger fish while the lighter rod will make the most of every other fish that comes along. Each and every fight is transformed into a much more memorable experience, which has surely got to be good and is certainly a lot more sporting.

It is also better on the fish. Winding them in at high speed does them no good whatsoever since it interferes with their ability to breathe at the very moment when they are straining to put more oxygen into their muscles to try to get away. Slower and smoother gets the job done just as well with the added advantage that the fish have a better chance of survival afterwards.

A lesser spotted dogfish typical of the stamp on the night with most of them weighing just under two pounds.

The next bite, on the Eurocaster, was not the determined pull of a dogfish. A shake and a rattle, pause, another shake and a rattle, gave way to a steady pull and a different style of fight from the pull down, have a breather, pull down again fight from a dogfish. This fish pulled away continuously, squirming backwards all the while I tried to pull it forwards so as to reel it in.

It turned out to be a silver eel, weighing about a pound and a quarter, which I returned so quickly that I forgot to take a photograph. (Sorry about that!) You could tell that it was a silver eel rather than a conger by the fact that it had smaller eyes, the lower jaw protruded beyond the upper and, most noticeable of all, its dorsal fin started further back along its body than that of the conger, which starts a short distance behind the head.

I caught a few more dogfish and whiting, sometimes two at a time on the Nexave, but by now the clouds overhead had formed into an ominous black mass and the wind had picked up considerably. I could have stayed and caught a few more but, even with my waterproof gear and a warm, comfortable hat on, I didn't much fancy the conditions.

It will never win any fashion awards but warm clothing is a must in the winter, even when you're only after dogfish!

My young companion was also off but we were both quite happy. We'd had a few fish and, though I probably enjoyed the fights a bit more, this particular night from the doldrums month of March had turned out, instead, to be a very pleasant evening. Certainly I thoroughly enjoyed it, which was down, in no small part, to the appeal of light tackle fishing. It just transforms the sport available!

Chapter Nine – Spinning and Plugging

Spinning – casting out and retrieving an artificial lure that spins and flashes as it comes in, thereby imitating a prey species to fool potential predators – has been around for a long time. We know, from historical references, that people in the 17th Century used to make their own minnow styles of lures for trolling for pike and salmon but the way in which such lures were mentioned suggests that artificials were likely in use for a long time before that.

The Victorians were certainly fond of them, using metal bladed spinners all around the world to catch a variety of predatory species. I remember watching an obscure television programme where an Indian Maharaja laid out for the presenter box after box of spinners that he had inherited from his great grandfather and which he was still using to catch mahseer today. All of the lures had been handmade by craftsmen and were still in immaculate condition, no doubt lovingly, or at least diligently, washed and polished after use to prevent the setting in of corrosion.

Today, a lot of people love spinning and, with the high tech materials available to make ultra light spinning rods, you can have a lot of fun with the fish that you catch. Personally, I'm not so keen, primarily because it's a very 'busy' method which can be a little intense. I like to take things at a slightly more leisurely pace, preferring the float or the fly, the former because I love to see it dart underwater and the second because the unique style of casting is more challenging and the retrieve usually more leisurely. You get time to visualise what's happening under the water, which is great considering the variety of retrieves available for experimentation.

But that's just me and, as I have mentioned before, that engaging in active imagination, that visualisation, is a major component of the styles of fishing that I most enjoy. However, I also recognise that, when your time is limited and you don't want to bother with bait, it's really easy to just grab your faithful spinning rod, slip on a fixed-spool reel, pop your tackle box of spinners and lures into your haversack and head for the coast. You can be fishing within minutes and catching from the very first cast, well, at least if the fish are there and, of course, if you're lucky!

It is a method that can be used at a very superficial level, with a small variety of spinners, plugs and rubber lures, or it can be explored in much greater depth, especially considering the huge range of lures available for people to buy.

Many people start with a rod capable of casting spinners from 21 – 35 grams, possibly up to 42 grams. This is strong enough to cast heavier spinners and a lot of plugs - thicker bodied lures designed to imitate small fish. It also lends itself to casting larger plastic lures fished with a weighted head or unweighted lures fished 'Carolina' style behind a weight. As an added bonus, they are also great rods for float fishing with bigger floats – say for when you want greater distance or when targeting bigger species such as bass, pollack and wrasse.

Lighter rods – say with a casting range of 10 to 23 grams – are also used for mid range spinning with such rods great for smaller species such as mackerel, herring, garfish and scad. Even lighter rods are available for LRF (Light Rock Fishing) work.

For all of these rods, there is a wide range of lures available but, on the whole, you can scale down your selection to a number of classic patterns designed to catch a variety of species.

Spinners

Basically these are metal bodied lures designed to rotate behind a swivel, hence the term spinner. The metal should be highly reflective so as to catch the light when you retrieve, thereby imitating the flash and play of light on the smaller prey fish that the spinners are designed to suggest. Some patterns don't actually spin and so are technically mini-pirks, metal lures with the hook, or the mount for the hook, moulded into or passing through the whole of the metal body. Very small to medium-sized spinners and pirks, because they are made of metal, are sometimes referred to as hard lures and so put the 'hard' into HRF or hard rock fishing.

Some useful spinners…

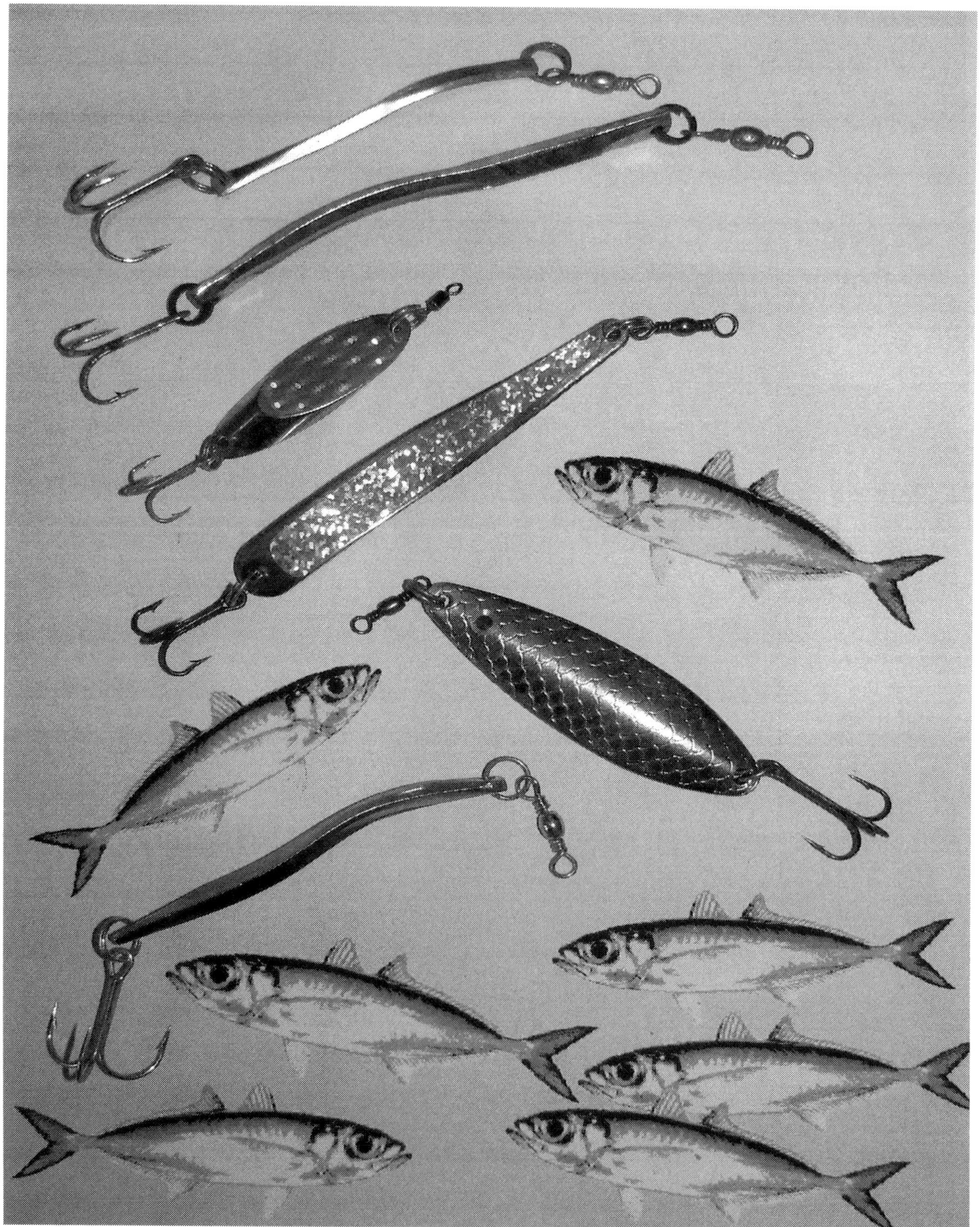

A variety of spinners that have worked well for me, especially the German sprat models (top and bottom) and Dexter patterns (third one down). I tend to carry a few models in a range of different sizes rather than lug around a vast assortment of what are often very similar lures. Toby and Koster spoons are also worth including with silver my go to colour.

Some useful pirks...

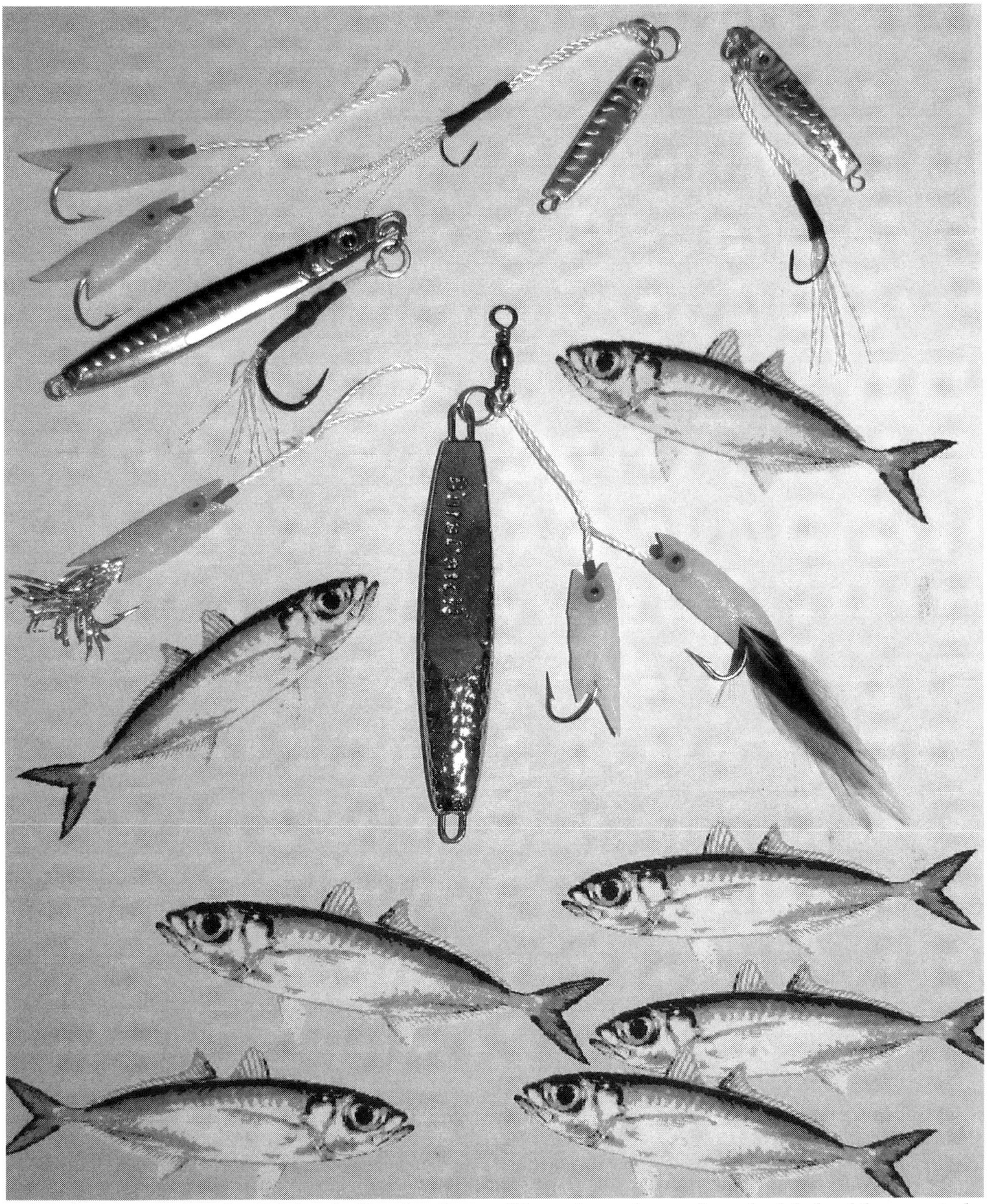

Mini pirks tend to be fairly similar in shape. These have been rigged with braid mounted assist hooks to help reduce tackle losses. In the past they tended to be rigged with a treble hook at the base of the lure.

A lot of people using smaller pirks now fit them with assist hooks fitted to the top eye of the lure. There are three main reasons for this:

1. The hook is less likely to get caught on clutter on the bottom than a similar pirk fitted with a treble at its base.

2. Many people are under the impression that fish nearly always target the head of their prey, believing that the hook is therefore in a better position to connect to potential predators.

3. A hook mounted in this way is easy to decorate, with the added bling swinging around and acting as an added visual attractor to your target species.

Every spinner has a different action and it is worth experimenting with your retrieves until you find what works best. German sprats can be deadly when a steady retrieve is alternated with side to side slashes while spoons seem to work best when you experiment with different speeds, slowing down and then accelerating to tease a fish into taking. Dexters, on the other hand, tend to work in different ways for different species. Bass seem to like a fast retrieve while mackerel often take them on the drop, especially if you pull them swiftly up towards the surface and then let them drop back at their own pace while you count them down through the water.

Pirks, by contrast, are designed to be fished in jerks and flutters, working them just off the bottom or at whatever level the fish are feeding. Pull them up quickly then let them drop down at their own pace. Repeat until you find the fish, which can make a successful pirking trip really hard work, especially if you are in a boat using some of the very big pirks that have been designed for cod, pollack and coalfish!

Plugs
These thicker-bodied lures are designed to imitate the swimming actions of small fish as they wobble, dive or surf across and through the water. Many of them are fitted with diving vanes that control the depth to which the lure descends. Generally you reel faster to go deeper and slower to fish near the surface. Others, known as poppers, have open, filled-in mouths that throw spray in front and behind of the lures as they are pulled, in jerks, across the surface. Bass, in particular, seem to like them with chugbug patterns often very successful. For myself, I love the sight of a bass exploding through the surface of the water as it homes in upon the plug.

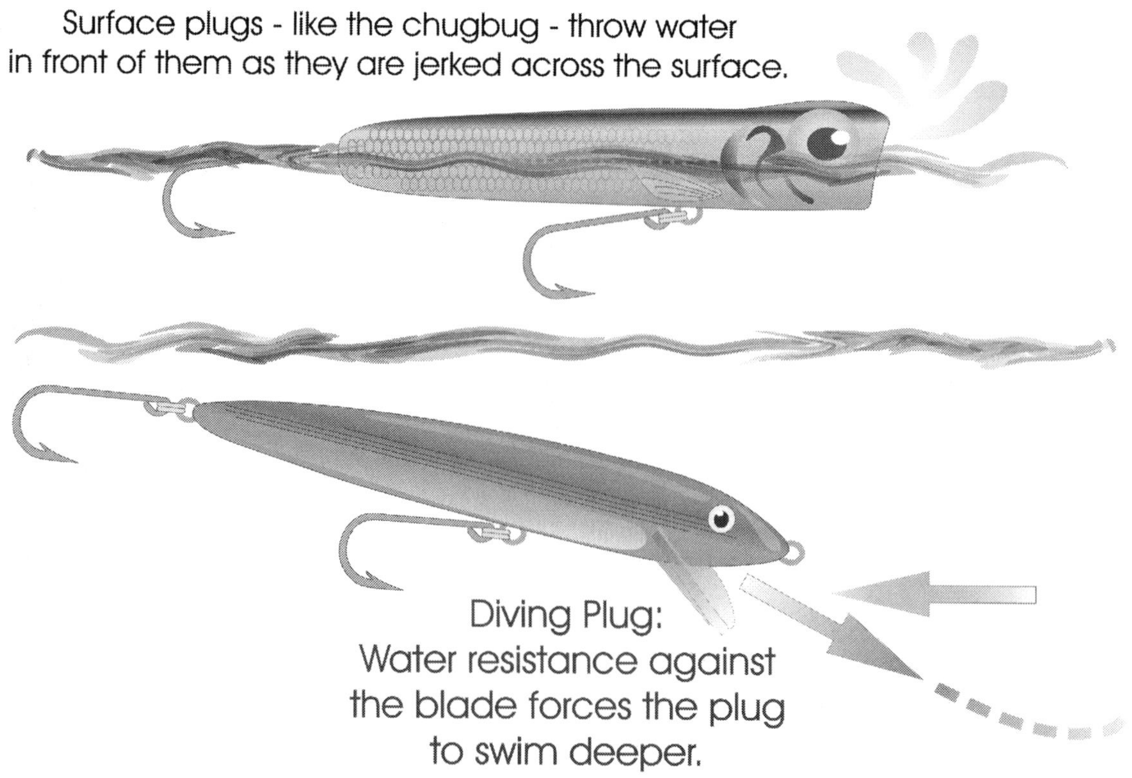

When the fish are feeding hard, I prefer to replace the treble hooks on plugs with singles, which do far less damage to the fish.

Apart from fishing from rocks, headlands and piers for bass, plugs can also be very useful for species such as mackerel. During the Autumn, most years, we get a short window of opportunity, near to where I live, when mackerel chase shoals of sprats close to the shore. They try to corral them in areas of shallower water and hit them in an absolute frenzy. At such times you can catch them on large flies, which is magic, but generally this is rendered impossible by the sheer numbers of other anglers that come down to fish for them. You simply don't have enough space to cast and, if you tried to, the fly line and hook would be extremely dangerous for other people. It's just not worth the risk unless, like me, you can find a few places which are well off the beaten track and where you can fish by yourself.

Spinners, at such times, do okay – and can be cast without difficulty when the fishing area is busy - but silver plugs simply excel. Every cast sees them repeatedly attacked with the larger plugs often sorting out the best and the biggest of the fish available.

Plastic Lures

There is a huge range of plastic lures on the market today, ranging from tiny sandeels to larger fish patterns such as shads, not to mention the worms, crabs and assorted other species that are starting to appear. Larger plastic fish patterns are often matched to weighted heads designed to match the body shape – like the hugely successful Fiish black minnow pattern - while smaller patterns can be fished on weighted jig heads. The latter, however, are generally too small to be cast by themselves on anything other than LRF (light rock fishing) and HRF (hard rock fishing) rods.

High tide at Hopes Nose – just as the rod bends into yet another mackerel on spinner.

Personally, I always carry a few spinners and plastic lures in my haversack, even when I am concentrating on float, just in case. I remember on one occasion, fishing with a friend of mine called Norman, when we had float-fished with no particular success for a period of several hours at Hopes Nose in Torbay. Discouraged, we were about to give up when, all of a sudden, the water in front of us exploded with thousands of mackerel harrying fry on the surface. The two of us exchanged glances then hurriedly whipped off our float tackle and tied on a spinner instead, in this case cebar metal spinners that are based upon the German sprat style of lure.

"We'll have to make this the last cast,' I said, some ten mackerel later. Ditto thirty mackerel later and, finally, the last cast was completed as mackerel number eighty one vainly protested its passage to the shore.

One thing that is worth bearing in mind, when the mackerel are shoaling in this particular manner, is that it is a good idea to take the treble hook off the spinner, or the plug, and replace it with a single. This is especially important when you are returning the majority of the fish that you catch. I will often take a handful of mackerel for bait but, when the fish are feeding hard, you can find yourself returning literally dozens to the water. At such times I will also use a pair of pliers to crush the barb on the hook, which reduces even further the possibility of damage.

So, on this particular occasion, why did the spinner work when float tackle failed? Basically it was because the mackerel were fixated – preoccupied – upon the smaller fish that they were targeting. Their normal feeding habits had been suspended because of the abundance of food available. They were chasing the fry to the surface and then taking them, at speed, in very shallow depths. Spinners could imitate the movement of these prey fish very well while the bait presentation afforded by float tackle – generally wafting around at a particular depth - couldn't. Okay, so I could probably have switched to bubble float and a fluorocarbon trace, working the bait through the top layers of the water but, at such times, even then I would probably use a plastic lure with the bubble float instead of bait.

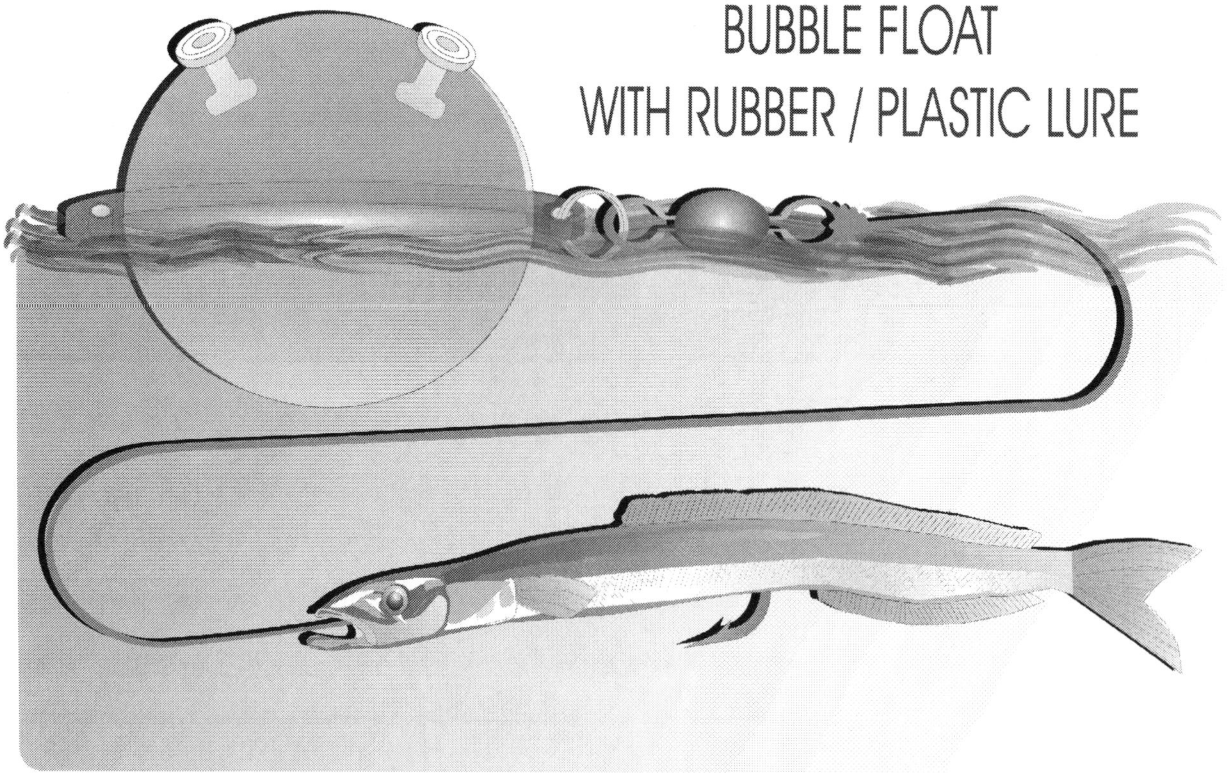

Bubble floats not only provide weight for casting but also enable you to work a plastic lure through the top layers of the water – a terrific strategy when mackerel, bass or other predators are harrying small baitfish at the surface.

The key thing to spinning is to always have it in the back of your mind, together with a few items of tackle in your tackle box, so that you can put it to good use when the occasion demands. Last year, for example, when I was fishing off the breakwater in May, leger and float-fishing had produced absolutely nothing. A few baby wrasse came up on a bight rig but, even then, there was little doing. I had, however, popped a few of the smallest Wildeye naturalistic sandeels into my bag, just in case, so I put one onto a six foot fluorocarbon trace, tieing it to the swivel on one of my wire-mounted drilled bullets before working it slowly along the bottom just to see what would happen.

For location, I decided, since nothing much had happened over the weeded area, to walk to the end of the breakwater and then cast to the sand at the very edge of the rocks. Sometimes some quite large shoals of fish can gather at such places, especially, at this time of the year, herring so it can be a useful place to try.

First cast produced a tentative pluck which then became stronger as the first of several herring had a go at the eel before being properly hooked and then landed. Now all right, sport may not have been great – herring are quite a small fish after all - but at least I was having some while the other anglers around me remained fishless.

Perhaps, at this point in time, a quick glance into my spinning box might be helpful, outlining why I carry the items that I do.

In relation to plastic lures, I carry some Marakyu Isome worms for wrasse, yellow, white, deadly nightshade and red rubber eels, especially red gills, for pollack and bass and Wildeye naturalistic rubber eels for herring. I carry dexter, toby and cebar spinners for mackerel and a couple of chugbugs and diving plugs for bass. In terms of accessories, I carry a few wire mounted drilled bullets, some drop shot leads and a spool of either six or eight pounds breaking strain fluorocarbon trace depending on where I am fishing.

I also make sure that my tackle box is worm-proof – to prevent it being damaged by the oils which some rubber lures contain – while the Marskyu Isome worms are kept in a separate, leak-proof container filled with the fluid that they came packed in. This stops them drying out and becoming rigid and useless.

All in all, it's not a lot to carry around but, over the years, this small selection has not only prevented many a day from ending up fishless but has transformed some of them into red letter days in my diary instead! It is a case of being prepared, especially when the unexpected happens and the predatory instincts of your quarry suddenly kick into overdrive. At such times, when other methods fail, spinning can make all the difference.

Chapter Ten – Fly Fishing

Mention fly fishing to the majority of people and they picture an angler wading in the midst of a tranquil river or gracefully casting at the side of a picturesque lake stocked with trout. Few immediately associate it with the sea despite there being a number of species and situations that lend themselves to this style of fishing. It is probably the least used weapon in the armoury of the light tackle sea angler.

And there are a number of reasons for this; the casting requires skill, distance is limited and there are far more locations around the coast where fly fishing can't be practiced successfully than there are places where it can be. Why on Earth would you bother?

But then, one day, you happen to be at a place where it all comes together and the reasons suddenly start to make sense. When you see the rod arch over as the fly is taken, when you feel the direct pull of your quarry with nothing between it and the end of your rod but the line, when every subtlety of the fight is transmitted directly to you, then you begin to understand. It can be a revelation. It certainly was for me the first time that I hooked a fish upon a fly and, from that moment on, I was as hooked upon the method as the fish upon the line.

For me, in whatever I do, if it is too easy then it doesn't really capture my interest. I like to feel that the fish that I catch are the direct result of all my preparations and planning bearing fruit, where everything is coming together, and fly fishing, especially if you practice it in the way that I do, is probably the most extreme example of this philosophy. I design and tie my own flies, work out places and opportunities carefully and then have to rely upon a successful cast to put it in front of the species that I'm after at the time.

But, if it works, what a difference! I think that the closest an angler can get to fly fishing using other techniques is LRF (Light Rock Fishing) but even this is somewhat clumpy by comparison.

The first time I tried fly fishing, I was a teenager, one living at a time when rods were far less efficient than the ones available now and where the line, instead of falling in graceful, limp coils, snarled its way around every possible obstruction in stiff, unyielding clumps. I had no one to help me with the casting, the gear was pretty miserable to use and the results as abysmal as anyone watching could have easily predicted. I felt extremely self-conscious and, to be frank, it put me off to the point where it was years before I tried it again.

But, when I did, I did it slightly differently. I practiced casting in a field until I felt that I could get a reasonable distance and I spent a little bit more money on the line, purchasing one that was a lot softer and more manageable to use. Then, when I went and tried the outfit out at the side of the breakwater, I caught herring, mackerel, pollack and even, to my surprise, greater sandeels, or launce as they are also known, including a giant sandeel weighing almost half a pound. It was really good fun.

I was still pretty rubbish at casting though – that only changed when I bit the bullet and paid for the services of a professional coach, spending a few hours and a bit of money that transformed my casting altogether. From that moment on, with a bit more practice, everything changed.

Get things right and fly fishing can be a devastating method, putting fish on the shore under conditions when other tackle just can't compete. I remember on one occasion, following the bass up an estuary with the flooding tide, when they were hitting sandeels in only six inches (15 cm) of water. My companion, who was armed with a dexter lure, was casting out and half-burying his spinner in the sand while my fly tackle, using a floating line, was able to delicately present my sandeel imitation right in front of their questing noses, prompting some savage takes. It was a great night, at least for me.

A lot of people, who have already tried fly fishing on stillwaters, bring their freshwater gear to the sea and that is fine as long as you rinse off and thoroughly clean the rod rings, the reel and the line afterwards. Saltwater is a lot tougher on fly reels than fresh and, if you don't look after your tackle, then it won't last very long.

That aside, there is nothing wrong with doing this, at least to start off. See if you like it before investing in dedicated saltwater tackle which, unfortunately, tends to be a lot more expensive. The biggest difference between freshwater and saltwater fly rods is the size of the fly that you can cast. A stillwater trout rod is fine for casting flies up to around two inches (5 cm) in length but, when you start using bigger flies, like clouser minnows for bass, then a dedicated saltwater rod will do the job a lot better and a lot more safely too.

I started with a trout rod and, for a long while, I used tiny red gills and delta eels instead of flies. There is nothing wrong with doing this and no reason why you can't experiment with other artificials, like the Marakyu Isome worms, for species such as wrasse. It can be good fun.

Nowadays, when I go fly fishing, I take three lines with me, including a floating fly line which I use for when the mackerel are chasing fry on the surface, in the evening for rising herring and in shallow harbours and estuaries for bass. I use an intermediate line for mackerel and garfish and a sinking line for deeper water marks for bass, pollack and wrasse. To these species, over time, I have added john dories, coalfish, scad and allis and thwaite shad with scad being the easiest of these species to catch upon the fly. However the first step is to get to grips with the cast itself.

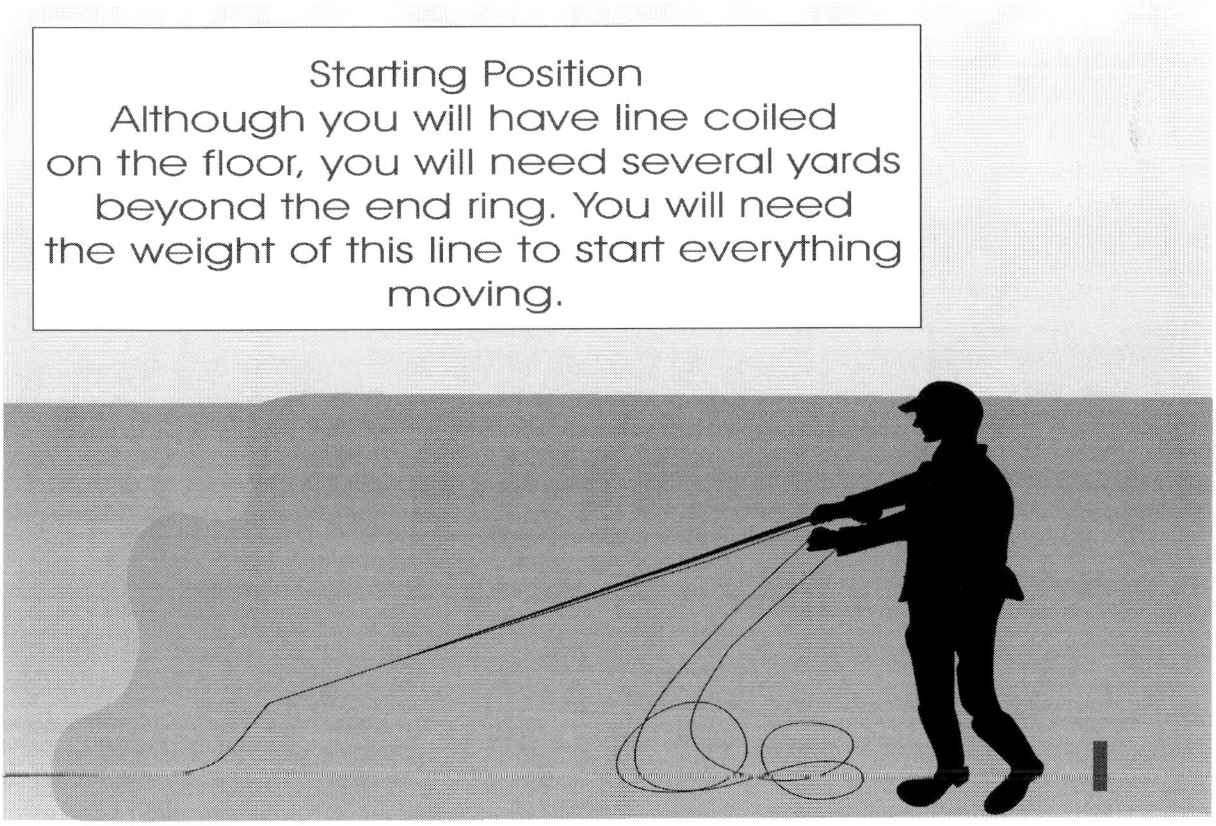

1. Before you start the cast, take a little time to get ready. You are going to need the rod tip pointing downwards - necessary to sweep as much line off the floor as quickly as possible - and you will need a good length of fly line out beyond the end ring. You need to bear in mind

that it is the weight of the fly line that makes the cast possible and, if you haven't got enough out, then nothing much is going to happen. You are still going to have coils at your feet but that's fine, they will be fed into the cast later as you put more and more line into the air.

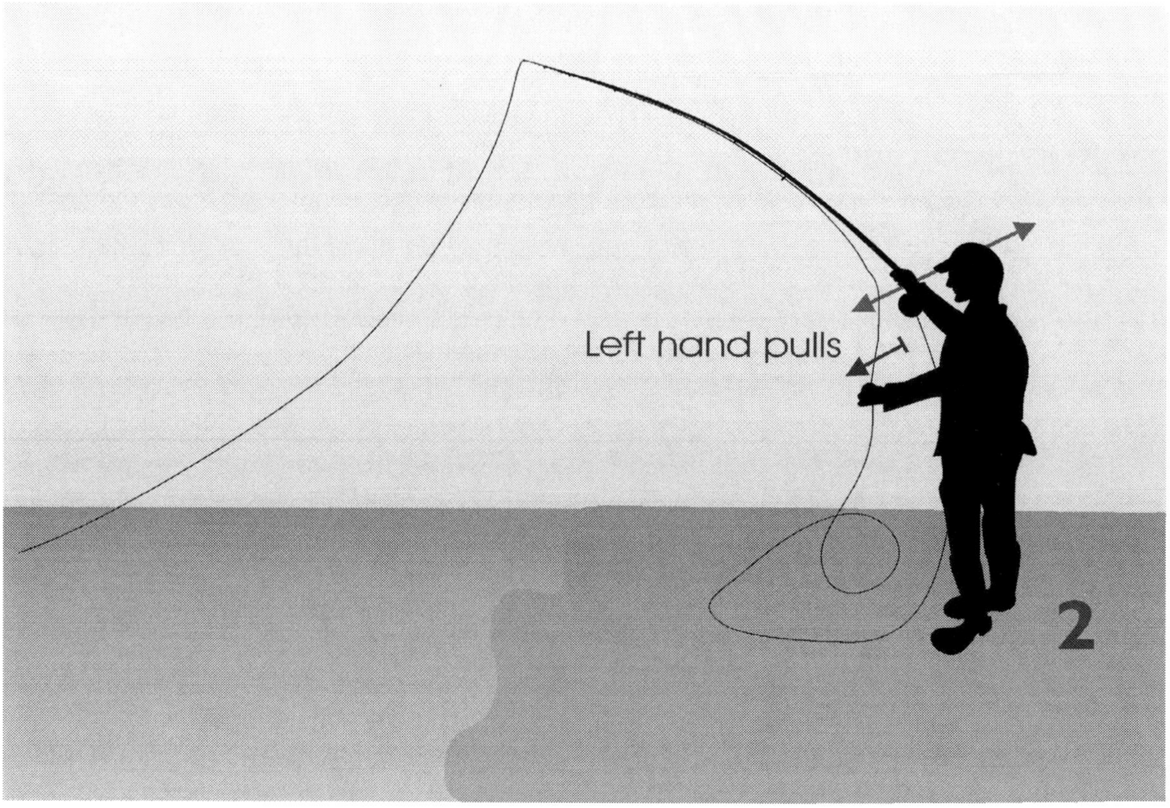

2. The next stage of the cast is to pick the line from the floor. You are going to need line speed if you are going to get any distance so sweep the rod sharply upwards, making sure that your right hand travels in a straight line as per the red arrow in the picture. This will get the line going in the right direction. Your left hand, which is holding the line, then accelerates it by giving it a sharp tug.

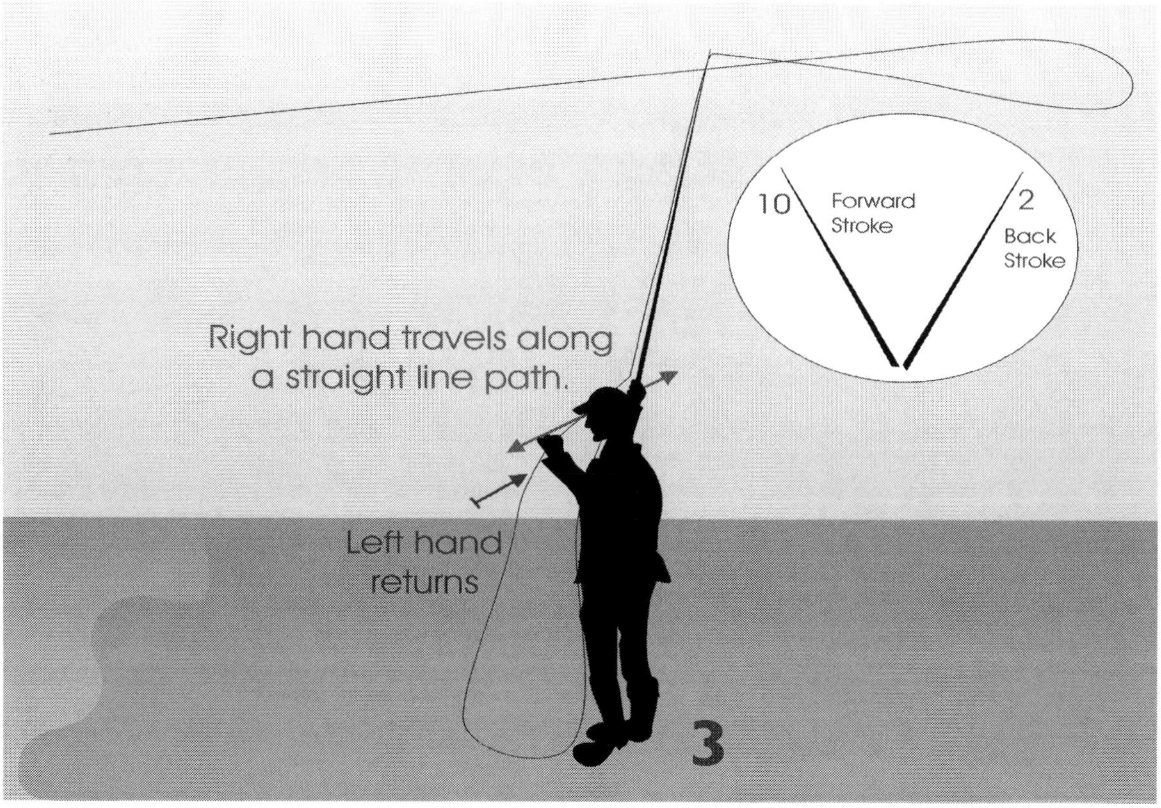

3. As the line straightens behind you, the left hand returns, ready to grip the line and give it another tug. You need to stop the line at about the two o'clock position then allow the line to straighten behind you, which will compress the rod before you start the forward cast.

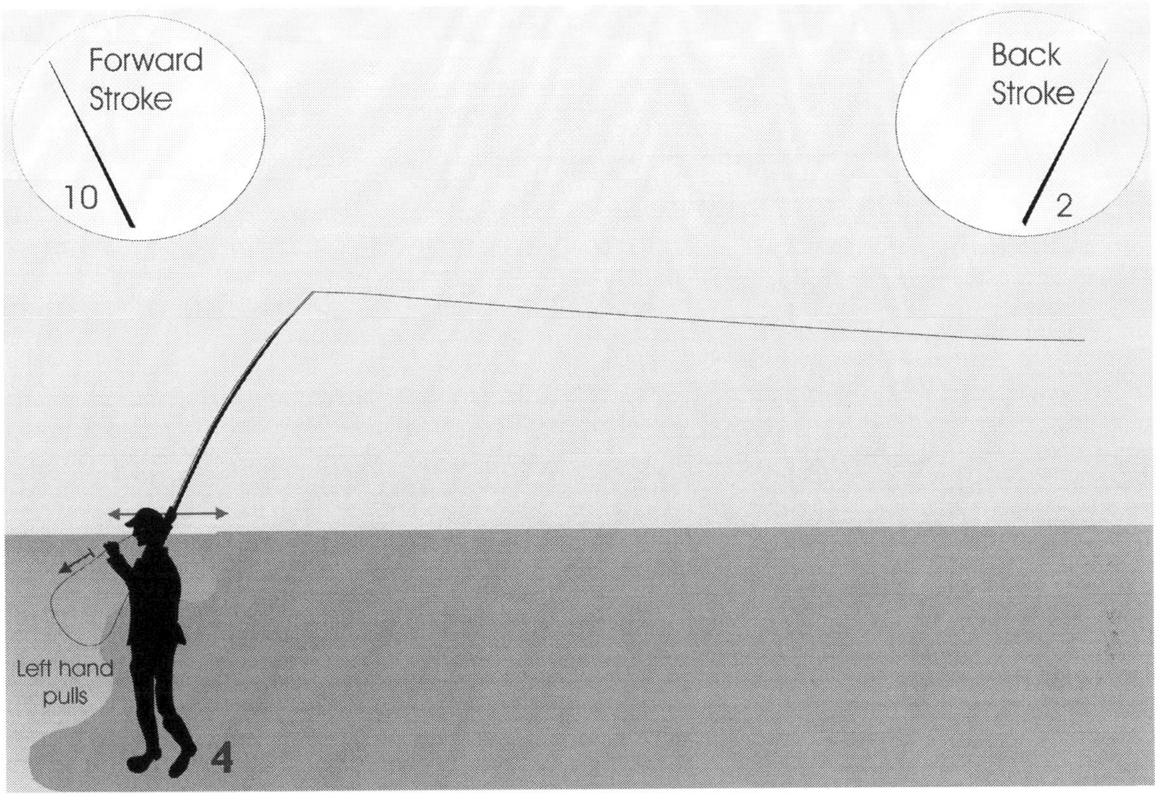

4. Once the line has straightened behind you, you need to start bringing the rod forward. This time, because you want the line to travel in a tight loop parallel to the ground, rather than falling towards it, the path travelled by your right hand will still be straight but it will now be at the side of your head. As the rod comes next to your ear, the left hand should be ready to give another pull to accelerate the line again and get it moving even faster.

When you are 'false casting' – moving the line forwards and backwards to generate line speed – the placement of the rod at the start and stop positions is crucial. Think two o'clock behind you and ten o'clock in front. When I was learning, I used to use 'tic toc' to help with my timing. The shorter the line, the faster the tic and the toc, the longer the line, the slower the tic and the toc, which is necessary to allow the line to straighten and be ready to be pulled again.

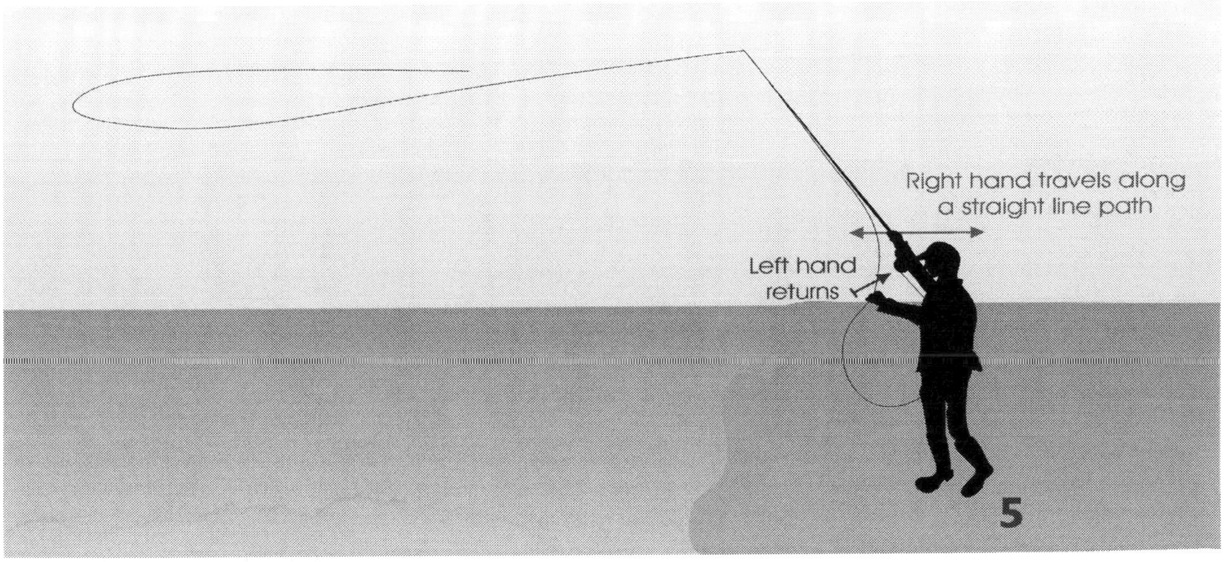

5. Your left hand returns ready for the next pull. With practice, you should find that only one or two false casts are necessary before you let go of the line completely on your final forward cast, ready to allow the fly to drop to the water.

Put the sequence together and it should look like this…

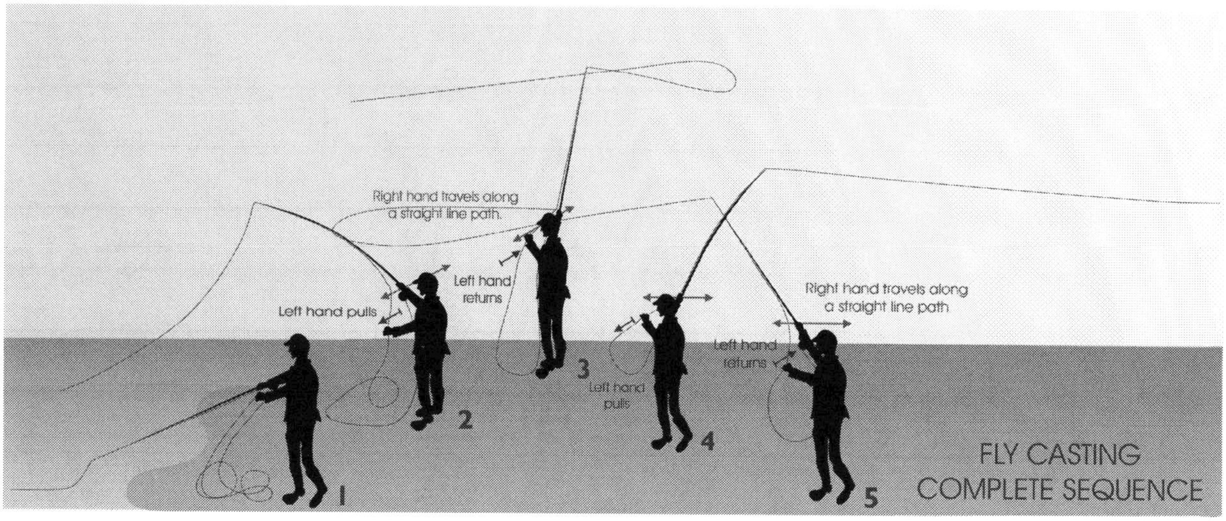

Over time, with a bit of practice, you will find that it all starts to come together but you can short cut this a little by taking advantage of the services of a professional angling coach. If you want to combine casting instruction with a fishing trip then I would suggest that you engage one who is at least a dual discipline coach – game and sea – or, like myself, a tridiscipline coach – coarse, game and sea – although, to be fair, there are very few tridiscipline coaches around.

Keep your eye open for free instruction too, especially on the events section of the Angling Trust website. From time to time, like many others, I offer free fly casting tuition on their behalf but I also do such events for Baywater Anglers, which is based in Torbay, as well.

If you would like to have a session with me, you can contact me via my website at www.devonfishingguides.co.uk. Don't be put off by the fact that it refers to me as Martyn Green though. When I started writing books on fishing, there were several other writers whose first name was either Martin or Martyn. I therefore wrote under my middle name – Lindsey – to help my books to stand out a little from the others.

Once you have got the hang of casting, you need to sort out a few flies. You can make your own, which I find extremely therapeutic and a good use of time at home in the evenings, or you can buy in a few patterns. A basic starting kit would be clouser minnows for mackerel and bass, some shrimp patterns for bass and pollack and some smaller flies for herring and scad. Personally I buy in some tiny sabiki feathers then detach the droppers from the trace, tie on a blood bight loop and fish them singly to a floating or intermediate fly line on a loop to loop connection. Mackerel, scad and herring really like these and it is an inexpensive way to start off.

As I have mentioned before, you can also experiment with plastic lures as long as you keep the size and the weight down. Over the years I have had a lot of fun with red gills – the 65mm size – with yellow and white good for pollack and purple, black and red good for mackerel. Isome worms are good for wrasse and flounder and tiny shad patterns good for mackerel.

Tying your own flies and using them to catch the species that you are after is probably the most satisfying experience but is really a bit beyond the scope of this particular book. Instead

I will be going into more detail on such matters within my next book – 'The Challenge of Fly Fishing' – where I will be crossing disciplines to describe how to catch coarse, game and sea fish. Fly tying techniques will be central to that manuscript, as will the philosophy behind both the patterns and the methods of retrieve used to target particular species.

Chances are, when you try fly fishing in the sea, that one of the first species that you will encounter is the ever obliging mackerel. These tend to hit the fly hard and give a good account of themselves afterwards.

I remember on one occasion, when I was driving home from work, I saw hundreds of seagulls waiting patiently on the surface of the water close to Livermead Beach in Torquay. Now since it was early September, my hunting instincts were instantly pricked by the thought that they could be waiting for the mackerel to chase sprats close to the shoreline, which often happens at this time of the year.

Fired up by this thought, I finished my drive and returned as quickly as I could with my fly rod, floating fly line and a few patterns of flies, including both my silver sprats and some epoxy resin bodied flies that had worked well for me in the past. The seagulls were still waiting patiently on the surface of the water – so I was in time for whatever was going to happen – and there seemed to be, if anything, even more of them than there had been on my way home.

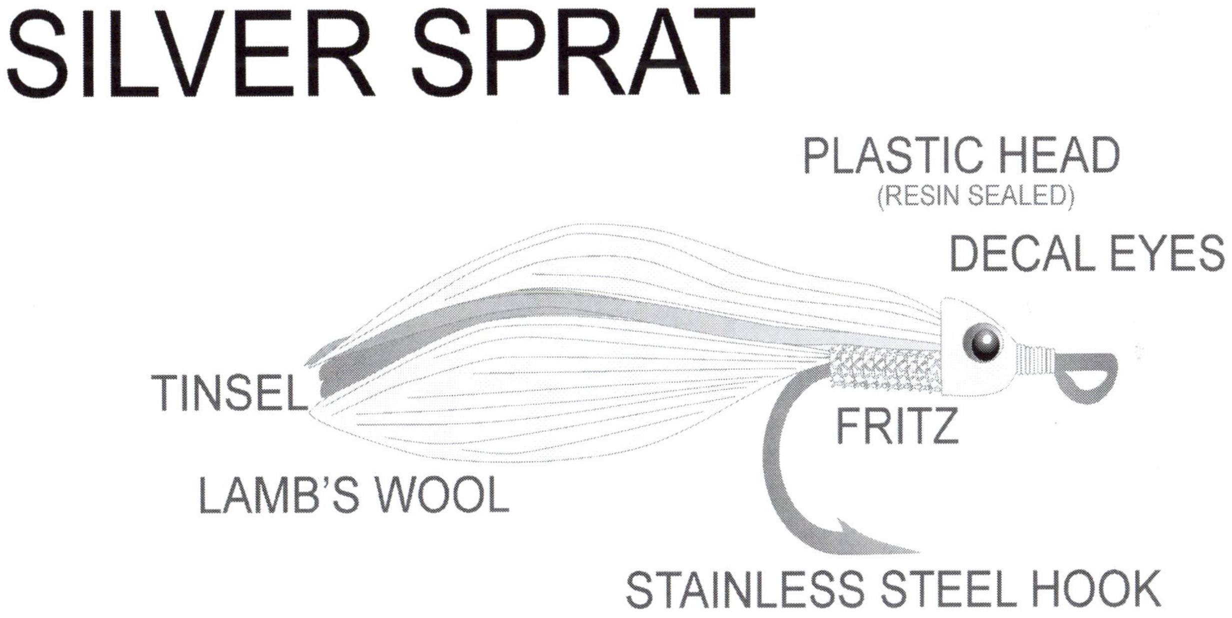

ANATOMY OF A FLY

Setting up quickly, I was just in time to see the seagulls suddenly hurl themselves aloft and give chase to a shoal of mackerel that had broken the surface, harrying the sprats that they were attempting to corral between themselves and the shoreline of the cove. It was mayhem – nature at its most brutal – but it was exciting too.

For a while the shoals were just out of reach so I had to be patient and wait. I tried a couple of flies – including the epoxy-bodied fly shown in the following photograph – and caught a couple of mackerel but, on the whole, nothing much happened until the shoal came in closer with the rising tide. Then, changing to a silver sprat – one of my own designs that is actually a pretty close match to the real thing – the fishing changed dramatically, the trigger being an eruption of mackerel directly in front of where I was fishing.

Sealing the heads of your flies with epoxy – like the fly in the picture – will help to make them last a lot longer against the sharp little teeth of our predatory species.

Casting into the midst of the shoal, I hooked up instantly, settling quickly into the fight only to experience a hard knock and then nothing - the fish had disappeared. Another fish picked it up but then, just as mysteriously, also came free. Somewhat baffled, I started to get a little frustrated as the same thing happened again and again until the fly was so close that I could see what was going on.

When it came into sight, nestled firmly at the side of a large mackerel's mouth, the reason for the knocks became obvious. A second mackerel, travelling at its companion's flank, darted forward, knocking into the first fish and freeing the fly from its hookhold before circling and taking it itself.

By now, since the rest of the shoal was close enough to see me clearly, the remaining mackerel slipped back into deeper water, leaving the one that was hooked to struggle gamely before being netted and drawn from the water. The shoal was simply feeding so heavily, in such a frenzy, that competition for the fly was leading to the constant hook-ups and knock-offs, with the final one taking the fly inevitably the one to be caught. It was superb fishing, albeit a little frustrating, but one of the best fly fishing sessions that I have ever encountered under saltwater conditions.

On another occasion, out with my family for a stroll on the Isle of Wight, a shoal of bass erupted from the water just in front of where we were walking, clearly harrying fry in only a few inches of water. Fortunately we were close to my car and I was able to grab my fly rod and flick a large chartreuse zonker just in front of the shoal. (A zonker is basically tied with a long, narrow strip of rabbit fur, in this case with the other elements of the fly being white and gold for a bit of extra visual appeal.) I then whipped it back right under their noses with short, sharp pulls that flared the long fibres and caused them to pulsate invitingly.

Fly fishing for bass in the very shallow water of a rising tide.

The floating fly line that I was using kept the lure near the surface and, within seconds, it was grabbed by a schoolie that went on to put up a spirited performance before being drawn to the waiting net.

Schoolie bass are terrific fighters on light tackle, putting a bend into a fly rod that just has to be experienced to be believed.

If the zonker hadn't worked, then I would have put on a little red gill, which would have been deadly under those conditions. However under the circumstances this wasn't necessary since this was the first of several, all of them returned promptly to the water and disappearing swiftly back to the depths from which they came.

When you do plan a trip, if you are going to be successful, it is likely that you will need to fish in either the evening or early morning. Predatory fish seem to be more active then and your chances increase accordingly. For me, I tend to target mackerel and bass in the early morning and evening, pollack and herring in the evening and scad in the evening and dark.

For most of these species, I use a fluorocarbon tippet – the line between the fly line and the fly – with three different strengths of line making up a staggered leader. The first three foot is 40 lbs breaking strain fluorocarbon, the second 25 lbs and the final four foot made up of 15 lbs breaking strain fluorocarbon, with all of the lengths joined by loop to loop connections. This may seem unusually strong but it is necessary to transmit the energy from the cast through the fly line to the fly, especially when you are using a big one.

Basically a well executed fly cast is similar, in some ways, to cracking a whip, albeit in a much more refined and well-controlled manner. The forces involved are severe and, with a poorly executed cast, could easily snap off the fly, especially if it is a larger one like a clouser minnow. However I don't bother with this arrangement for herring and scad, for which I use a tiny fly like a Sabiki lure or a small red fly, for which they also seem to have a preference. These flies are so small that I use eight to ten pounds breaking strain fluorocarbon throughout.

For scad, when I am fishing into the dark, I like to use a small fly with a luminous body, charging it with an ultraviolet light to emit a bright glow when it is in the water. Pollack will also take these flies but I tend to use sinking lines for them and, depending on the light conditions, floating or intermediate lines for the scad. The reason for this is that the scad will rise in the water, which pollack will also do, but the latter will tend to hunt near obstructions, which tend to be found nearer to the seabed than the surface. Scad, on the other hand, will come right up in the dark, especially wherever there is a light overlooking the water. Such places are well worth investigating, especially since they can be great places for herring too.

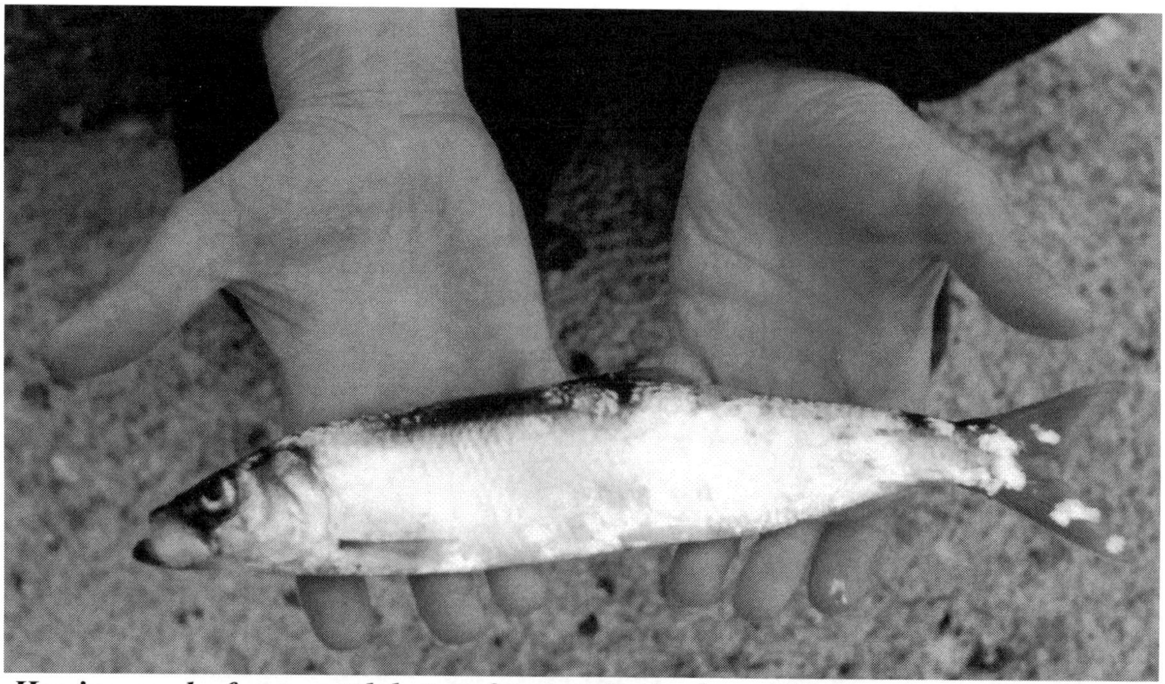

Herring can be fun to catch but, unfortunately, don't usually grow large enough to be interesting.

The movement that you give the fly and the speed of your retrieve will also be crucial to your success. You can figure of eight it in slowly or give it sharp little pulls to pulse the fibres of the fly. You can creep it in or you can tuck the rod under your arm and speed it through the water hand over hand. Each species will react differently. Wrasse will go for Marakyu Isome worms twitched slowly back on a sinking line – even in the middle of the day – but you will need a strong saltwater rod to cope with them. The same thing works for flounders, depending on your location, but bass will go for anything pulled quickly back through the water, as will mackerel, pollack and scad. By contrast herring will react well to a moderate retrieve.

To 'figure of eight' your line, I find the most comfortable way of doing this is to reach for the line with your finger and thumb, curve your other fingers over it and then close your other fingers on it one by one. Drop the line with your thumb and finger while reaching for it again and then drop the line from your other fingers while curving them over the line ready to close on it again. With a little bit of practice, you'll soon get the hang of it.

Another accessory that you will want to consider, especially if you are going to be using waders, is a line stripping basket. If you wade without one of these you will find that the current takes hold of your fly line and makes it really hard to cast again.

All in all, fly fishing can be a great deal of fun but do keep an eye on your surroundings, especially other anglers and passers by. Don't forget that your fly line will travel as far behind you as it does in front of you, which could be hazardous for others. That aside, I hope that the moment that you catch your first fish on the fly will prove as magical for you as it was for me. There really is nothing like it.

Mind you, if you do decide to adopt a light tackle approach, even without experimenting with fly fishing tackle, you will have some really exciting moments to look forward to, with every fish fighting to the best of its ability.

And that's why, for me, sea fishing with lighter tackle rocks!

25641570R00059

Printed in Great Britain
by Amazon